Hindu Thought and Carmelite Mysticism

This book is translation of *Pensée Indienne et Mystique Carmélitaine*, published by le Centre Védantique Ramakrichna, Gretz, France.

An earlier version of the translation appeared in various numbers of *Vedanta for East and West*, Bourne End, England

Hindu Thought and Carmelite Mysticism

Swami Siddheswarananda

Preface by
Christopher Nugent
Appreciation by
Swami Ranganathananda
Translation by
William Buchanan

MOTILAL BANARSIDASS PUBLISHERS
PRIVATE LIMITED • DELHI

First Edition: Delhi, 1998

ISBN: 81-208-1510-6

Also available at:

MOTILAL BANARSIDASS

41 U.A. Bungalow Road, Jawahar Nagar, Delhi 110 007
8 Mahalaxmi Chamber, Warden Road, Mumbai 400 026
120 Royapettah High Road, Mylapore, Madras 600 004
Sanas Plaza, Subhash Nagar, Pune 411 002
16 St. Mark's Road, Bangalore 560 001
8 Camac Street, Calcutta 700 017
Ashok Rajpath, Patna 800 004
Chowk, Varanasi 221 001

PRINTED IN INDIA

BY JAINENDRA PRAKASH JAIN AT SHRI JAINENDRA PRESS,
A-45 NARAINA, PHASE I, NEW DELHI 110 028
AND PUBLISHED BY NARENDRA PRAKASH JAIN FOR
MOTILAL BANARSIDASS PUBLISHERS PRIVATE LIMITED,
BUNGALOW ROAD, DELHI 110 007

Table of Contents

Translator's Note

This is quite a literal translation. The Swami's quotations have been translated from his French rather than from some standard English translation. This should make it easier to follow the Swami's thought.

Swami Siddheswarananda did not identify all his quotations, and some of the identifications he did have proved to be inaccurate. I have tried to find accurate identifications for his quotations, but I did not succeed in tracing all of them.

Sanskrit words are used frequently in the lectures. I have provided a glossary for those words except for those explained in detail in the text. I have also provided a glossary of names of persons and books which might not be familiar to some readers.

I should like gratefully to acknowledge help I have been given by the following people: Swami Yogeshananda of Eternal Quest for locating some quotations; and Edouard Cohen of the Ramakrishna Vedanta Centre, Gretz (France) for correcting errors in the translation; and to Prof. Linda Scott for Proof reading.

William Buchanan

Biographical Note on Swami Siddheswarananda

Swami Siddheswarananda was born into the Royal Cochin Family in 1897. Some of his teachers in school introduced him to the teachings of Sri Ramakrishna and Swami Vivekananda, and while a student at Madras University he was initiated by Swami Brahmananda. He joined the Order of Ramakrishna in 1920 and took *saṁnyāsa* (final vows as a monk) from Swami Shivananda. Swamis Brahmananda and Shivananda were direct disciples of Sri Ramakrishna.

The order of Ramakrishna was founded in 1903 by Swami Vivekanada to carry on the work of his teacher, Sri Ramakrishna. The Order is unique among monastic orders in India in that its members perform social service work (running schools, hospitals, clinics, serving in emergencies, somewhat like the Red Cross). In 1937 the Swami was sent to France to found a centre for the Order. He carried on his work even during the dark days of World War II. His lectures at the Universities of Toulouse and Montpellier and at the Sorbonne have been published. The lectures in this book were given between 1949 and 1953 in the amphithéâtre Richlieu (Sorbonne) under the auspices of the Centre de Recherches Philosophiques et Mystiques. The Swami passed away in 1957.

Letter of Appreciation

Ramakrishna Math
Domalguda
Hyderabad
30 January 1992

Swami Siddheswarananda had, as his father, been a prince of Cochin State, Kerala. He was intensely humorous and kind-hearted. He had the good fortune to receive spiritual initiation from Swami Brahmananda, the first president of the Ramakrishna Order and a prominent disciple of Sri Ramakrishna, and blessings from Swami Shivananda and other fellow disciples of Swami Vivekananda. One year after he started the Mysore Centre, I joined his Centre as a Brahmachari in 1926. I was 9 years in Mysore with him and another 3 years with him in Bangalore till he left for Paris to start that Centre. Everybody, the poorest as well as the richest, in Mysore and Bangalore, loved him. He had a great sense of humour. Though endowed with keen intelligence, he was simple like a child. I received my best intellectual and spiritual training during my life under him. I was there in Karachi to receive him when he came to India from France for the first time at the end of the Second World War in 1946, when I was the head of the Ramakrishna Mission, Karachi. After a few months of his tour in India, I bade him farewell to France at Karachi. His early death has been a great blow to Vedanta work in France and to the Ramakrishna Order as a whole and to me personally.

Yours in the Lord,
Swami Ranganathananda

Preface

In 1889 the English poet Rudyard Kipling could write, "East is East and West is West and never the twain shall meet." I rather doubt that he would write that line today.

We are increasingly aware that the world is an interdependent reality—and a mysteriously interdependent reality. Symptomatic of the change, and well before, let us say, Americans had discovered the Toyota, was the presence of a Bede Griffiths in the East and a Swami Siddheswarananda in the West. "Nothing human is alien," wrote the ancient Terrence, and our corollary might well be "Nothing divine is alien." Nothing truly divine.

William Buchanan and Motilal Banarsidass Publishers have themselves made a signal contribution to the emerging spiritual universe by making Swami Siddheswarananda's exemplary book accessible to an English-speaking audience, something for which I have long hoped. I first chanced to encounter his *Pensée Indienne et Mystique Carmélitaine* (1974) in the course of researches into "the Mystical Doctor," St. John of the Cross (1542-91) at the Bibliotheque Nationale, Paris, some years ago. Immediately I found myself charmed by the work, an unusual blend of insight and solidity. Here was no ingenuous tract ecstasizing over the latest *avatār* but an equally engaging work of real discernment. Here, then, was evidence that nothing truly divine is alien.

My own special interest among the Carmelites of golden age Spain is John of the Cross, collaborator with St. Teresa of Avila, mystic extraordinary and master of prayer, in the stormy spiritual and moral reform of their community. St. John of the Cross is himself among the most universal of mystics. His poetry, for example, has been compared to that of Rumi. There has already been interest in his peculiar affinities with Zen Buddhism. Therefore, Thomas Merton, probably John's foremost disciple in our century, could affirm: "Frankly, I would say that Zen is nothing but John of the Cross without the Christian vocabulary."*

The Swami, master of Vedānta, is an acute interpreter of the Mystical Doctor. He brings out, and brings out for the first time as far as I know, how John can be holomorphic, to enlist the phrase of Raimundo Panikkar, with Indian religious thought. John, he greets even as "the Patanjali of the Occident." Indeed, the Mystical Doctor is seen as an embodiment of *Rāja-yoga*, a synthesis of *Jñāna-Bhakti* and *Karma-yoga*. And John's spirituality is indeed all these things, an all but indistinguishable mixture of gnosis, agape and, despite his personal preference, active service. It goes without saying that the Carmelite has no doctrine of, say, the *cakras*, but he does have, I believe, some essential correspondences. For example, his radical disciplining of the senses is to open the renunciant to liberation and awakening. Moreover, contrary to a rather modern aberration of the cult of pure experience—if indeed, there can be such a thing—faith is essential. But this faith is a prefiguring of wisdom.

What the Swami has given us is in fact a contribution to wisdom literature, and the flowering of a wisdom literature around the world is corroborative that nothing divine is alien. At the same time, Siddheswarananda is no partisan of some mystical melange. While he illuminates the common ground of two great spiritual traditions, he is loathe to dissolve facilely the historic differences. And so while he can affirm that Ramakrishna had an experience of Christ, he demurs from claims that this is a specifically Christian experience. Again, he does not homogenize John and Shankara, though I would venture that John issues, ultimately, in a *Christian* equivalent of Advaita. In *The Living Flame of Love*, for example, the Mystical Doctor mysteriously ones even "fire" and "water".

Siddheswarananda suggests to me how world spirituality can be not only interdependent, but mutually elucidatory. May the light shine through his book to a large international audience.

Univesity of Kentucky **Christopher Nugent**

[1] *Springs of Contemplation: A Retreat at the Abbey of Gethsemani*, ed. by Jane Marie Richardson (New York: Farrar, Straus, Giroux, 1992, 177)

Abbreviations Used

AMC.	:	*The Ascent of Mount Carmel*
BG.	:	*Bhagavad-Gītā* (The Song of the Lord)
Col.	:	St. Paul's Letter to the Colossians
Cor.	:	St. Paul's Letter to the Corinthians
DN.	:	*The Dark Night of the Soul*
Gen.	:	Genesis
Gal.	:	St. Paul's Letter to the Galatians
GM.	:	*Ramakrishna, the Great Master*
Gospel	:	*The Gospel of Sri Ramakrishna*
HB.	:	*The Book of Habakkuk*
Heb.	:	The Letter to the Hebrews
Matt.	:	The Gospel According to St. Matthew
Num.	:	The Book of Numbers
Ps.	:	Psalm
SC.	:	*The Spiritual Canticle*
SS.	:	*The Song of Songs,* which is Solomon's
St.	:	Saint

1

Hindu Thought and Carmelite Spirituality[1]

My intention in this series of lectures is to show you some points of agreement between Christian mysticism, particularly Carmelite, and Hindu thought. This study in no way claims to be definitive: it aims only to offer some degree of clarification to the comparison of these two currents of religious thought.

Some thirty-five years ago, when I knew nothing about Carmelite mysticism, I became acquainted with the writings of Brother Lawrence of the Resurrection. Christian thought was much in vogue then, and our monastery was regularly publishing certain texts. Thus it was that I happened to read the sixteen letters of Brother Lawrence,* which had just been translated. They seemed to give me just what I needed at the time. Fresh from the university, competent in intellectual matters only, I had been given upon my arrival at the monastery practical tasks I was unfamiliar with: cleaning floors, doing dishes, cooking, etc. Though I accepted these tasks with joy, I was nevertheless having a hard time

---

[1]This lecture was delivered at the Sorbonne on January 15, 1949. It was titled "Pensée Indienne et Spiritualité Carmélitaine."

*An asterisk after a word indiates that it is explained in the glossary.

reconciling them with the contemplative life I had originally desired to lead.

Reading Brother Lawrence was an overwhelming experience which brought me peace. Anyone who knows the life of Ramakrishna can perhaps compare the life of this lay brother with the life a young illiterate servant—later known as Latu Mahārāj*—led near the Master at Dakshineswar. Brother Lawrence, in fact, knew how to reconcile the most rigorous manual labour with the highest states of contemplation, the ideal of the *Bhagavad Gītā* realized in concrete form. This life confirmed for me the truth contained in our traditional teaching.

"When ten people asked me ten things at the same time," said Brother Lawrence, "I was as calm and collected as I would have been in front of the Holy Sacrament." Like the disciples of Ramakrishna, for whom we nourish so much admiration, this humble Western monk had realized in himself the harmonious union of the spiritual and the active life. His actions, far from being extraneous to his contemplation, issued from it as its fruit; and contemplation itself, far from being a flight from life, actually prolonged it. This equilibrium between the leisure of Mary and the activity of Martha, which we find in Brother Lawrence, awoke in me an echo, as it were, of the *Bhagavad Gītā*:

> He who sees inaction in action, and action in inaction, he is wise among men, he is a yogi, and he has performed all actions. (IV, 18)

Speaking today, so near the place where Brother Lawrence used to work, Rue de Vaugirard, I am happy to offer him the homage owed to an *upaguru.**

Since my days in the monastery, I have become acquainted with numerous religious orders in France. I have had the privilege of visiting the Grande Chartreuse, as well as three Trappist monasteries, and I spent some time in a Dominican convent. Father Bruno courteously lent me excellent documentation on the Carmelites and permitted me to spend a few days in the monastery of Avon. Having known at first hand something of the monastic life in the West, I wanted equally to understand its inner, spiritual life; so I studied carefully St. Teresa of Avila, St. John of the Cross, St. Teresa of the Child Jesus, and Sister Elizabeth of the Trinity.* Those writings revealed to me a genuine kinship with Hindu mysticism. I must say, however, that I will not speak here from a religious standpoint.

Religion erects barriers between men because it rests on concepts which are provocative slogans and rallying points. That is why there cannot be amity between particular religions if one considers doctrinal and theoretical values. The word "spirituality," closer to our ideas, is of a more universal order: it designates this life which expands slowly in the deepest part of ourselves and which is indefinable because it is ceaselessly renewed. All its manifestations (symbols, ideas, beliefs) are only its changing envelope, according to the different doctrines and notions which men form of God when they think about the problem of salvation.

But if we take the word "religion" as signifying human efforts to realize the highest level of consciousness, a transformation of being, then we discover at the innermost recess of the different religions, however different outwardly, a true oneness of aspiration, a completion in the sense of a blossoming of the soul—a conversion, in short, which transforms the animal that was man into a divine being in whatever religion he belongs to, to the extent that his religion does not consist in vain discussion, polemics, and subtleties.

That conversion is the fruit of spiritual aspiration; religious practices to which humans adhere are only expressions of that aspiration on the material plane. That expression, furthermore, can take numerous forms. How could we demand that doctrines and beliefs, so different, should be translated by the same rites and sacraments? (I know that this point of view cannot be accepted by Christians.)

I am often asked, "How can you subordinate doctrine to religious experience and the transformation of character—all things which are, for us, from doctrines we already possess, which is to say from faith?" My reply is simply that it is never by insisting on questions of principle and doctrine that one augments love and understanding in anyone. Those principles, by setting up boundaries, have much more tended to exclude and divide. They have created neither love nor mutual comprehension. If, on the other hand, we consider the lives of the great mystics, we see in them a kind of spiritual realization which makes them all brothers in the same outpouring of sympathy for humanity. Forgetting doctrinal barriers and theoretical divergencies, they are in love only with Truth under whatever form they have discovered it; and this love shines forth and attracts as no dogma ever will. That is why I think the word "spirituality" has for all people a greater attraction than the word "religion" has.

It is above all in Carmelite Mysticism that I met this inner thrust of the soul which characterizes Hindu thinkers. Is it because this mysticism, entirely turned towards the interior activity of the soul, had no interest in exterior conquests and the proselytism so foreign to the spirit of Hinduism? Or, as some have said, could Carmelite mysticism have unknowingly received the imprint of Sufism? Then there would be a true link between Carmelite mysticism and India through the intermediary of Spain.

Whatever the interpretation may be, I will try, nevertheless, to establish parallels on three points of comparison: I will study for each the contents of consciousness in the course of three successive moments:

1. Prayer (the Discipline of Purification).
2. The gift of self to God accompanied by suffering.
3. Union with God.

1. PRAYER
(THE DISCIPLINE OF PURIFICATION)

In the course of this study, in which I will dwell especially on the psychic contents of experiences, I will have occasion to point out great differences concerning some fundamental notions, such as those regarding the soul and God. These differences do not in any way involve the contents of the soul; they are important only because, leading to different interpretations, they generate incomprehension. For instance, the idea we have of a mother in India is not the same as yours in the Occident. The expression of feeling, also, is different: in India we do not embrace; we bow while joining hands. Can one say, however, that love is not the same in the two continents?

We do not have your Cartesian way of considering the faculties of the soul as issuing from a principle opposed to matter, namely, mind. Mind, for us, is completely outside determinations, and all appearances in this world, whether under a subtle or gross form, are part of prakṛti, that is to say, the creative energy of the Divine.

The soul—*jīvātman*—seen as the envelope constituting its internal organ, is thus a material portion, however subtle, of the universe (*prakṛti*). Brahman is for us the immutable basis of all existence; this notion cannot be related to that of God, because Brahman is without attributes—solitary (*kevala*). One might better translate your notion of God by *Īśvara,** the Lord of the Universe; or *saguṇa** Brahman, the Brahman with attributes.

Once more this distinction which we must make (lest we be reproached with syncreticism by trying to reconcile irreconcilables) in no way prevents us from recognizing an underlying identity of aspiration.

Perhaps you know how Ramakrishna would illustrate the kind of discord which exists on the point between theory and practice:

> Two people, having begun to argue about the nature of God, were coming to blows, when a passer-by, seeing that the situation was getting dangerous, thought it would be good to intervene. 'You have perhaps seen God?' he asked one of the disputants, once he understood the nature of the problem. 'No,' he replied. 'But surely your father saw him?' 'No more then I.' 'Then your grandfather?' 'Not at all.' 'Probably it's the same for you?' he said to the adversary. 'Why do you bother arguing about something you have neither seen nor heard?

Such is the impasse to which one is brought when one depends only on theories. Mystics, on the contrary, deal with us on the level of experience; we can relate to them.

You will object, perhaps, that this experience is different; it is on the ground of character and reactions in the face of life's difficulties that we will find the same peace, the same love.

But I am of the opinion that one can find a mystical fraternity even at the interior of experience, if one is content to examine the psychic contents of those states of union. The mystic needs dogmas and beliefs only when an explanation is asked of him, for the mind can understand only by inferring the universal from the particular. Thus it would be better to practice religious truths than to spend time arguing theories.

We will begin today with an exercise considered fundamental for religious life in both hemispheres: Prayer.

Prayer, as you know, is nothing other than an ardent supplication to enter into intimacy with God, a means by which we present Him our credentials, as it were, so that He will authorize us to enter into His dwelling place. Christians consider that there is no better formula of introduction than our Father, and St. Teresa advises us, while chanting the words, to meditate on their sense in order to disengage the ideas which that great prayer contains. You should read attentively chapters 27 through 42 of *The Way of Perfection.* This prayer, leading us to different degrees of collectedness, realizes in us a veritable inner transformation.

We in India have the same exercise, which we call *japa.* It consists in repeating the Name of God. "Rama is the strength of the weak," sings Sūradass.* There is a difference, however: in India one repeats the sacred Name only after having received an initiation.

Initiation (*dīkṣā*) plays a role of the first importance in our Indian tradition. There are several kinds: that which confers *saṁskāras** (latent tendencies) in creating certain dispositions for spiritual life; here the role of the sacraments is very important.

There are also initiations which consist, by the *mantra dīkṣā*, in an influx of spiritual strength, through a Mantra or sacred formula, which the guru transmits to his disciple when he judges that the latter is sufficiently ready. The repetition of the Mantra is supposed to integrate the spiritual aspirant with Divinity, for the Hindu believes in the objective presence of the spiritual being of his God at the interior of the Name communicated. This presence, by means of repetition, becomes integrated with the individual, who becomes a same substance with it, rendering him more spiritual than he was.

This notion is rather new to you, because for you the encounter of man with divinity occurs only in the Holy Sacrament. It is there that you find the Christ, the objective Presence; and prayers, rites, all ceremonies are for you only the means of purifying yourselves in order to permit you to approach the Holy Table in a more perfect condition.

We have also the idea of the concrete presence of God, such as you have, in the *pratīkas,** a word very badly translated by "idols." Just as in the Catholic rites the priest invokes the Presence of the Lord in the bread and the wine, so the Hindu invokes His Presence by means of his rites, either in certain images, or in *yantras** and *maṇḍalas*,* or even, as in the custom with the *tāntrikas** of the left (*vāmācārins*) in wine.

Each time that the worship is done, this invocation must be made in the form of an *āvāhanam*; that is, it must bring forth the real Presence of the Divinity, followed by a communion which also differs from yours. This is not the place to discuss it. I want to insist here on communion through the *mantra*. All other communions can be considered as exterior forms beside it, simple concrete preliminaries leading to a subtler communion of the aspirant with the Divinity whose Name has been communicated by a qualified guru. They are thus optional, whereas the *mantra* is truly the sound which carries Divinity.

Certainly, one can see the *mantra* as an ordinary name, a word in print for instance; but that will not make you a true initiate. In order to be initiated you will have to receive it by way of apostolic succession; that is to say by a guru who will himself have received it from a Master, going back until you reach Divinity.

To repeat the *mantra* is to communicate with the spiritual force contained in the Divinity. The *mantra* is thus indeed an objective presentation of the Divine under the vibrant form of sound.

And, just as you consider that the Lord in His Presence, Power, and Essence, is present in the sacred Host, so we consider that the *mantra* encloses Divinity. Differing in the *pratīkas*, where His Presence needs to be invoked each time, the Lord remains in the *mantra* as in tabernacle of perpetual Adoration.

The responsibility of the worshipper asking initiation is exactly that of the Christian who desires to take communion. He must first purify himself, if he has committed some fault, by expiatory rites; for without an ardent love for God, repetition of *mantras* is inefficacious. These conditions realized, the disciple who repeats the *mantra* is certainly transformed.

"Do you think the name of God is such of trifling matter?" Ramakrishna used to ask. "God is no different from His Name. Satyabhāmā tried to balance Kṛṣṃa with gold and precious stones, but could not do it. Then Rukmiṇī put a *tulasī*-leaf with the name of Kṛṣṇa on the scales. That balanced the Lord" (*Gospel*, p. 386).

And he added:

> When one comes to believe in the Power of the holy Name of God, and feels disposed to repeat it constantly, neither discernment nor exercises of piety are any longer necessary.

> All doubts are appeased, the mind becomes pure. God Himself is realized by the Presence of His holy Name.

And finally:

> Whoever pronounces the Name of God, under whatever form, voluntarily or involuntarily, will in the end find immortality.

Let us try now to see how this transformation is realized, which, as we have seen, is as much a fact of *japa** as of Christian prayer: to borrow the vocabulary of St. Teresa, a prayer, like *japa,* acts on the "Powers." (Thus she calls the three faculties of the soul: will, memory, and understanding.)

The will, while still weak in the aspirant, is, by prayer or *japa,* put into contact with a great spiritual figure by whom it is, as it were, awakened. The love, which is then exchanged, channels the energies which were previously dispersed.

But according to the words of St. Teresa of Avila, the love is not yet strong enough to "hurl its arrow into the heart of divinity." For that, a purified energy is needed, and it is here that memory comes into play.

Memory exerts itself in the midst of all our faculties in union with imagination. Drawing us towards the sensible world, memory provokes in us, by neglecting the essential, all the failures of our will. A will which has not been purified cannot be strong, for it does not know from what unconscious region of itself forces some day will surge up and sweep away the work which had been begun (the *saṁskāras* of the past).

Our true will can thus be awakened only during the night of the senses and the mind, when the "powers" are asleep. At that moment memory finds God again, and that Intelligence which we call *buddhi** begins to awaken. Then the soul seems passive, because all its strength is utilized to concentrate better on uniting more closely with the Divine.

> As long as the mind remains attached to consciousness of the external world, it sees material objects and resides in the physical sheath of the soul (*annamayakośa*: the sheath of food).
>
> When the mind is directed inward, it is as though one closed the door of the house and penetrated into the apartments inside. The mind goes from the gross body to the subtle body, from there into the causal body and finally

> attains the ultimate causal state. Having reached that point, he plunges into the Absolute of which nothing can be said. (Gospel, p. 604)

These words of Ramakrishna, very close to those of St. Teresa, describe quite well the ascent of the soul which occurs in the course of prayer.

One sometimes hears it said that the Hindus consider the state of union with God to be a simple performance of the human will obtained almost automatically thanks to that kind of gymnastic called yoga. That is a serious error.

The method of yoga is a simple method of purification: it has as its end lifting the obstacles which bar the way of the aspirant, preventing him from realizing the fullness of consciousness to which he aspires.

It goes without saying that no mental mechanism, however perfected, can attain God. How could the unlimited, the extrasensory (*atīndriyam)*, the measureless, possibly enter into the limited framework of our means of apprehension, (*manas,** *buddhi,** *citta,** *ahaṁkāra**) none of these psychic instruments can, by itself, bear the divine message.

Like you, we say the Grace of God alone permits us to know Him. The Truth is a flash which illumines the *buddhi.* We say that truth is *buddhigrāhram,* grasped by it, but is not an intellection. It is an illumination. The mental faculties do not intervene; it is when they are at rest that Truth is revealed: *pratyakṣāvāgamam.*

In the ordinary state of consciousness the superior *buddhi* is the point of intersection where the light of the Supreme Consciousness is refracted in a multitude of rays, thus making the one appear indefinitely multiplied.

This multiplicity is further augmented by that image-creating faculty of the soul (*saṁkalpa* and *vikalpa*) which projects the mind towards multiplicity.

The *citta** is the seat of all memory, and it comes with the *ahaṁkāra,* that is to say, the sense of the ego, in order to appropriate for itself, through the thread of mental images, all that the inferior *buddhi* decides to think about. It is only when the wanderings of the mind are suppressed by the control of memory and understanding that the *buddhi,* the seat of pure decision, can reflect the divine.

> Only the Supreme Intelligence (*bodha svarūpa*) can realize the Supreme Intelligence, said Śri Ramakrishna, and he added: That is the sense of the expression, 'God is unknown and unknowable.' (*Gospel*, p. 729)

The superior *buddhi* in question here does not belong to the manifested world; it is not part of our mental apparatus. It is in us in a causal state, the Supreme Consciousness unaltered.

These *Sāṇkhyan* categories correspond rather closely to the division which St. Teresa makes of the faculties: the two sides of the mental process seem the same. If someone burns up a bird's nest, the bird flies about. I takes shelter in the sky, said Sri Ramakrishna. "Similarly when the mind is no longer conscious of the external world or the body, the soul soars into the Supreme Heaven" (*Gospel*, p. 782)

Illuminated by this supernatural intuition, the soul which returns from that state radiates peace (*śānti*).

2. SUFFERING

The second point which we have to study is suffering. The peace which the saint achieves is often preceded by a long hard struggle. With you, as in the Orient, suffering is the gate which opens the spiritual way by permitting us to discover very near us the presence of God. In the two hemispheres, however, we have different ideas about it. For you, inheritors of Greek thought and especially Hebrew theology, life retains almost always a sad, tragic resonance. Religion is conceived only by participating in the sufferings of the crucified Man-God. Religion is enclosed in a history of sin and a particular perspective of redemption: without the suffering of the Son sent by God, who could be saved? Reduced to his own power, man cannot find the way of salvation. Only the coming of Jesus, his love, his sacrifice, accorded men what they had sought in vain: redemption.

From that moment on, considered as cooperation with the work of the Cross, suffering appears to you bathed in a special halo. I recall witnessing in 1938 at the Church of the Trinity a sight which moved me very much: it was Good Friday; I saw a little girl at the foot of the Cross weeping and kissing the feet of Christ.

This attitude towards suffering is quite unfamiliar to us. We can understand it, but we have a different way of looking at it. The dominant note in Hindu thought is that of Peace. There is no tragedy in our literature; in our dramas, the denouement must be happy and leave the spectator filled with serenity. Our religion, though founded on the notion of sacrifice—the world is the fruit of the great sacrifice of puruṣa: "I am myself the Lord of the sacrifice *adhiyajña*, O Pārtha," says the Lord in the *Gītā* (IX 24)—admits neither the notion you have of the unpardonable sin nor that of the absolute necessity of a "new creation." I cite the words of St. Paul: "Do you not know that all of us who have been baptised into Christ Jesus were baptised into his death? We were buried therefore with him by baptism into death, so that as Christ was raised from the dead by the glory of the Father, we too might walk in newness of Life." (*Romans* 6:3-4) Nor does our religion admit the idea of the unity of the way which is thus opened by the divine Redeemer.

The keystone of Christianity, considered as a religion of salvation, lies in the bloody sacrifice of the Cross. For us Hindus, for whom the notion of sin is never that of an unpardonable sin, the bridges between men and God are never cut off. If the necessity of the coming of an Incarnation is established, it is because "vice abounds and virtue is on the point of succumbing." (*Gītā*). The ways to the divine are not blocked; they have simply become impracticable, and man's progress is therefore stopped. The Avatār is a messenger. "When the religious idea weakens in one part of the world, God sends his messenger to instruct men in the way which leads to Him (Ramakrishna).

Suffering in itself does not seem to us to possess a spiritual nature. We consider it the natural state which suits the impermanent compounds of which we are formed. If it enjoys in our eyes a certain prestige, it is because it permits us to understand better what factors constitute our personality.

All that exists, in fact, as a consequence of successive acts of compounding caused by desire (*kāma*). Desire, by projecting itself on material, ephemeral things, leads one to identify with them in an infinite search which makes one an incessant flow of successive unbalanced compounds.

Suffering is produced when this tension is brought to its maximum intensity. What happens most often, then, is that man, incapable of bearing that tension, makes himself break it by diverting his attention towards other objects. There exist for man various ways of consolation, from tears to the most elevated speculations. They are the crutches which permit man to continue to live in the same manner, by following other paths. Those crutches are necessary, and I would not think of denigrating them. I am not at all of the opinion of certain thinkers who would refuse man the consolation of any church. But I want to show you a higher knowledge suitable for highly evolved intelligences who want only comprehension. When man accepts bearing his suffering, thanks to that virtue with which he is gifted and which we call *titikṣā* (endurance), without trying to divert the potential of the accumulated forces to some activity which replaces them, he sees then the energy which, up to a point, was augmenting the tension of being, become displaced and begin to feed and illuminate his consciousness. The centre of perspective has changed, and the factors which composed his individuality disintegrate. Energy, abandoning transitory elements, turns towards the permanent. Being which is the base of personality, the Supreme Consciousness, the *Ātman.*

> And I know that I am the Knower in all Fields, O Bhārata; and only the knowledge of the Field and its Knower do I regard as true Knowledge. (BG, XII, 3)

Just as in a dream the *manas* ceases to be identified with the material body (*annamayakośa* and *prāṇamayakośa*), or as, in profound sleep, the *ānandamaya* ceases to identify itself with the *manomaya* and the *vijñānamaya*, that is to say, with the *manas* and the inferior *buddhi*; likewise here, when man consents to keep the attitude of a spectator, his mind, detaching itself from its exterior envelopes, attains the unmanifested causal state, he realizes then the experience of Being: it is said that he is liberated.

This experience necessitates great courage, for the will, engaged up to this point in sense experiences, must cross nothingness; that is to say, it must consent to break off all relations with the manifested and be satisfied with nothing. It is what happens in very rare cases, as for instance, after the death of a very dear one, in the course of the final stages of the sādhanā, when the will to live, detached from all material satisfaction and entirely concentrated on itself, "sharpened" (ekāgrita), returns to the source of Life.

All life thus passes through states of perpetual tension which make a long valley of misery engendered by the disappointments of frustrated desire. The tension can be virtual, like sickness in a latent state: the individual is satisfied. It is only when the sickness awakens, that is to say, in the moments of bitter suffering, that we are permitted to study it. Only the Sage, who has no more past and no future because he lives in the plenitude of Being, realizes that state which is beyond suffering and knows bliss.

> Let that be known as yoga, which is severance from the contact of pain. It is to be practiced with perseverance and with undaunted mind. (IX, VI 23)

Such is the reaction of Hindu thought when faced with the problem of suffering, suffering considered as the most authentic specimen of a life fragmented into multiplicity. It is in that confrontation with suffering that our intelligence is illuminated.

From the religious point of view, we can thus consider suffering as an ordeal which is sent by God with the intention of measuring our fidelity towards Him. "Do not leave me without suffering," Kunti, the mother of Arjuna used to say addressing the Lord, "for in happiness I would forget you."

For both Christian and Hindu, suffering produces a transformation. In offering his suffering to Christ, the Christian derives from it an elevation of consciousness which is already partaking of the Kingdom of Heaven. The Hindu, in trying to understand it, encounters serenity. In one case as in the other, through detachment, suffering leads us to make a total gift of our person to God. To accept it is to abandon body and soul to the divine will. "It is no longer I who live . . .," said St. Paul (Galatians 2:20). This world is unreal, full of suffering; know that and consecrate yourself entirely to Me," says the *Gītā*. It is by this abandonment of self to the divine will that suffering is truly the way to reach God.

3. UNION WITH GOD

The third point of comparison is spiritual experience, immersion into the Divine. Several people who know the different states of spiritual experience in St. Teresa of Avila, for instance, and then get to know Ramakrishna or some other Hindu mystic, try to find parallels. This way of thinking prevents us from realizing perfectly the different positions of these mystics. To reduce these different positions to unity is to create artificially a universal which crumbles under the slightest critique.

If we seek similarities, we must know that it will be impossible to find them in the different doctrines or in the different theological interpretations which we have been given from each side. The intellectual and psychological backgrounds of the Christian mystic and the Hindu mystic are completely separated. When I permit myself to say that, in the psychological content of their experience, one can discern certain similarities, I do not imply that "All that is the same thing." None of us has the possibility of penetrating the interior of the ecstasies of a St. Teresa, a Ramakrishna, or any other mystic. Those saints belong to an ideal world which can be appreciated only by one who has access to it.

It is in the transformation of character that we can note similarities. All the truly great mystics lived in Love; they saw the world and they conducted themselves towards it in a manner totally different from the manner of us poor humans. They all become, to use the language of the *Gītā, sthitaprajñas* (men of firmly established intelligence). Then there is no more need to say "it's all the same thing." We recognize immediately in all mystics, of no matter what country, the same appearance of kinship.

If we compare the ecstasies of St. Teresa, for instance, with the different stages of *savikalpa samādhi,* we must not forget that the way of seeing according to Hebrew revelation is almost the antithesis of the way of seeing according to the Vedas. Having said that, it remains nevertheless true that the human psyche, whatever doctrinal food has nourished it in the course of its formation, presents some similar aspects. "All jackals cry the same way," Sri Ramakrishna used to say. After having tasted of the same realities, the mystics make the same harmonies heard. Basically, they all speak of the same union. And just as during the assimilation of a given food, the same biochemical processes take place whatever the formation of the physiological system may be, likewise whatever the religious formation may be, the soul in its relationship with the Divine assimilates in the same manner.

You know, perhaps, the totally materialistic interpretation of spiritual experiences which modern psychologists (such as Leuba* or Morton Prince*) have given, reducing them to glandular psycho-physiological origins. Without entering into the exaggerations of any particular point of view, we Hindus also have from time immemorial catalogued our rigorously controlled experiments. Modern psychologists can be reproached for not having studied the religious individual directly. They can be reproached for letting their judgments be vitiated by certain presuppositions regarding mystical experience. In general, you in the Occident, fearing to get lost in the subtleties and confusion of the mystical state, prefer to take objective guide marks for measuring them; thus one of those guide marks for you is the communion with the divine by means of the Holy Sacrament.

The mystics are exceptional beings who, in the course of this very life, receive by divine grace certain means of knowledge which the ordinary man does not possess. Since seeking that grace often leads through states of disequilibrium, the mystics are not encouraged. Lacking, perhaps, datum sufficiently rigorous for formulating the laws of mysticism, you prefer to take shelter behind Doctrine, which you see as offering more security. All that is required is a life that is just according to the commandments of God and the rules of the Church. The Holy Sacrament permits you to introduce an objective criterion into mysticism; for it is there that the encounter is made between the human and the divine. Christian souls must not seek outside the regular practices of the Church; they would risk falling under the influence of the great Tempter.

Faith, with us, is far from being a matter of organization and permits a multitude of doctrinal viewpoints. Some of those viewpoints do not even include any religious concept. Thus, we have been led to seek outside of any particular doctrine a ground of experiential understanding; that ground is yoga, which defines different states of consciousness in relation to different practices and which makes of meditation a science which is physical and mental at the same time. It goes without saying that meditation is only state of preparation for the divine contact: as we have seen, the mind is incapable of attaining the inexpressible. All mental exercise, however disciplined it might be, will never be able to attain that from which "words fall back without having been able to win Him." Contemplation of the divine is an inborn grace, but it remains, nonetheless, true that the different stages of preparation fall, insofar as they are mental dispositions, under the jurisdiction of yoga.

It goes without saying that exterior manifestations, such as levitation, halos, or miracles, are phenomena which can be part of yogic training. Ecstasies in their different degrees can be studied from the viewpoint of the levels of consciousness which accompany them, levels of consciousness which would be the expression of the awakening of those centres of power which we call *cakras.** The word "ecstasy" signifies literally the state which one attains when one is outside of oneself. To designate that state we use the term *bhāvasamādhi*, which comes from the root *bhū*, meaning 'to grow,' 'to become.' Growth here consists of an expansion of consciousness, which characterizes entrance into more and more vast regions of reality. It is equally a matter of getting out of the self to fuse with the divine Self.

Now I would like to speak of a misunderstanding on this subject. When a Hindu reads a study on comparative mysticism, such as that of the Reverend Father Garrigou-Lagrange,* he is rather shocked to learn that pagans cannot penetrate the mystical way beyond the fourth mansion.[1] In Catholic doctrine, in fact, only the Holy Sacrament can render possible an objective and real contact with Christ and permit the initiated soul to enter into the fourth mansion. Canon Lépée,* in his remarkable thesis on St. Teresa, insists on the objective character of this experience. He writes: "Jesus Christ has not given himself to us, since he ascended into heaven. He has never descended to earth to communicate with men except in the very Holy Sacrament."

The visions of St. Teresa, however, though they are not imaginary, are nonetheless not endowed with that character of objectivity to which you Occidentals give primacy. Although coming from the Holy Spirit by the Grace of the Lord himself, they do not possess the value which, in the eyes of a Christian, the objective act of communion, indispensable for salvation, possesses. When

[1]Saint Teresa in *The Interior Castle* describes the soul through a metaphor: a castle in the form of a transparent crystal sphere containing several rooms or "mansions." The first two correspond to the purgative way and the ascetical life; the third and fourth correspond to the illuminative way and bring the soul to the threshold of the mystical life; the last three are concerned with the unitive way or the mystical life.

a worshipper is blessed by the grace of these visions, what counts above all for him is that he does not deviate from Christian Faith, Faith maintained by communion, confession, and other religious exercises. Each of his experiences must conform to Christian Faith; the slightest deviation from that faith suffices to make his experience and the theory he derives from it to be considered as heretical; a position exactly the inverse of ours, where the theory never enters except to support the greatest number of facts. In mysticism, with us, experience is superior to theory, and if, from the Christian point of view, a Hindu not having faith—I use this word in the sense the Catholic Church gives it—nor the means of expression authorized by that faith, cannot go beyond the fourth mansion, then it is completely legitimate that we Hindus, who have another conception of God and for whom the mystical experience is not limited by any *a priori* dogma, can accede to the highest state of Union.

We do not accord the same importance as you do to objectivity. Certainly for us also the world exists, but man does not occupy the same place on it that you have him occupy. In the Christian way of looking at it, the world is a theatre where historical drama is played out, represented by the adventures of the descendants of Adam with sin. Space is closed, time is a static and empty decor, and man is the first actor of a drama in which the divinity participates. For the Oriental, space is like Brahman, without limits, and time itself is the creator of multiplicity. This thought is anything but anthropocentric; for it does not cease to consider this infinite panorama of the cosmos across which beings, more or less liberated, evolve. Nothing there is static, nor does anything possess an absolute reality. In the waking state what exists is divided into objects and ideas, but the content of consciousness changes, as, for example, in the dream state, or in a mystical state where another world appears, divided in the same manner into objects and ideas.

All exists, like this *virāṭ** in its objectivity, this world of stars and planets disseminated in the immensity of ethereal space (*mahākāśa*); there exists also a world of ideas, the *hiraṇyagarbha*,* behind which the source and centre of all that is manifested holds fast, the supreme cause, *Īśvara*.* At the very interior of this world of ideas, the experience which you have could be at the same time objective and subjective. Let us take the example of a dream:

while it is occurring it seems to the dreamer as real, as though he were awake; it possesses an objective content to which one can oppose the mental reactions of the characters who participate in it, which we will call subjective. It is the same thing when an individual has the grace to penetrate into the world of ideas, in the mental cosmos: that universe presents, just as that of a dream, an aspect of objectivity. It is in no way less real, less objective, than the shrunken world of our sensibility, which in the brief instant of our duration, is cut to our measure.

Take the case of a dream I might have at 2 a.m., in which I have a conversation with Mr. X of Calcutta. In itself this dream is subjective, hence unreal; but suppose that at the same moment Mr. X in Calcutta has the same experience, which consists in meeting me in Paris in order to speak with me on the same subject and that we get to know the identity of our dreams. Our contact has thus indeed been, although ideal, objective in the sense that all took place as though we had truly met at an objective point in time and space. If our daily lives offer us this possibility, why not admit experiences of a higher order in the domain of ideas? According to our Hindu concept, there exist in the mental cosmos of great Beings, past Incarnations with whom worshippers can come in contact; and we say that this world, to which we can have access only by hard discipline, possesses still more objective reality than this poor world of the waking state which is so quickly limited.

Perhaps it will be easier for you to understand, in the light of this summary presentation of our Hindu thought, how we interpret the encounter of Jesus and Sri Ramakrishna. We will offend no one by saying that this was not a Christian experience of Christ, for Ramakrishna did not belong to the Church and consequently his contact with Jesus could not be objective if one understands by objective a normal experience in the waking state. The contact, although immaterial, nevertheless really took place. It took place in the manner of the immaterial form which Ramakrishna called *nitya-rūpa,* the glorified body. Those forms are eternal. You know perhaps how that vision took place. For some time Ramakrishna had been thinking very intensely of Jesus, when, walking under the Panchavati, he saw approaching him an extraordinary person, radiating serenity, who looked him in the eyes. He seemed to be a stranger: his eyes were beautiful and large, his nose a bit long.

Sri Ramakrishna, contemplating him and wondering who he could be, suddenly heard a voice in his inner depths: "This is the Christ who shed his blood for the redemption of the world and suffered agony for humanity. It is Jesus, the Incarnation of Love."[1] Ramkrishna lost consciousness and melted into that divine form. As in the experience of Soul, who also had never taken communion nor accepted any creed or belief, this was a real contact with the Lord. The grace of Jesus alone was sufficient, grace realized in the soul of the future apostle that opening of consciousness which was to transform the persecutor into a fervent disciple. The criterion of objectivity for these mystical experiences resides in the transformations which they effect. Those who receive the grace to enter into contact with Jesus, Rāma, Kṛṣṇa, or Buddha, experience a change in the very deepest part of their soul. "Truly he who has received one glance of divine love is blessed for the whole of his existence," said Ramakrishna.

Whether we be Hindu, Christian, Muslim, Parsee, Buddhist, or Jew, what we seek through the experience of the mystics is that radiance of love which transforms our life. It is in love that all the contradictions vanish, since for him who has realized it in his heart, there is no more diversity.

In presenting this series of lectures on a subject so rich in similarities, the prayer which I address to the Lord is the following: May He be kind enough to accord me the benediction of remaining in the course of these two currents of spirituality, bathed in the rays of love, which are freed from one another.

OṀ Śānti, Śānti, Śānti.

[1] This event, which occurred in November, 1847, is recounted by Swami Nikhilananda in his introduction to the *Gospel*, p. 34, and by Swami Saradananda in *Śri Ramakrishna, the Great Master*, p. 339.

2

Spiritual Practice

1. Askesis and *Sādhanā*[1]

The subject which we are going to treat now is askesis and *sādhanā* according to St. John of the Cross and Hindu spirituality. Askesis and *sādhanā* are two words which, taken in their broad sense, contain the same idea: spiritual life—more exactly, the manner in which spiritual life is practiced.

Why practice asceticism? Why practice *sādhanā*? Man, such as he is, finds himself in a state of disarray and disequilibrium; he perceives that he must improve. The aim of asceticism is a true transformation of being. The transformation begins when man can no longer remain in the condition in which he finds himself. Caught in a maze of contradictions, riveted by suffering, he desires to escape his condition and attain a level of existence where he would find only peace and happiness. That fortunate condition is called *śreyas* in Sanskrit. It encompasses everything beautiful and good in existence. It is spoken of in the Upaniṣads, especially the '*Taittirīya*,' as the supreme joy which is brought by the knowledge

---

[1]Titled "Ascèse et Sadhana," this lecture was delivered at the Sorbonne on February 19, 1949.

of God. That knowledge is *mano-ānanda* or bliss for the spirit and *prāṇārāma* or superior joy in the vital energy and *śāntisamṛddham*, impregnated in all its dimensions by peace. That state is the end which guarantees the validity of our spiritual life. But what must be done to attain that end? Would it not be an hallucination?

No! *Śānti* is Peace in all its plenitude, and the joy of *prāṇārāma* is incarnated in the lives of those great ones who had the courage to set out in search of God. It is not a bookish knowledge but a knowledge realized in the very stream of this life.

This knowledge necessarily begins with self-examination. We usually try to hide our weaknesses from ourselves; we do not like to remain alone and confront silence. The spectre of our intimate contradictions forbids us to emerge from the anguished state in which we are immersed. Fortunately we can find in our midst some who desire to break away from this impasse: they are the great lights-made-flesh: Jesus, Buddha, Ramakrishna, and others incarnate the purpose of this existence, and their unique existence illuminates our night. Like those stars which shine in solitude, they can seem strange to us, perhaps; but compared with what we are, in the abyss into which we have fallen, we discover that all Truth is in them, and we are obliged to turn towards their light.

They are the ones who have traced for us the ways of asceticism and have taught us what *sādhanā* must be. Whoever those great instructors may have been, the psychological course they set is the same, even though they take different doctrinal positions and make use of differing methods at the outset. Those instructors, delivered from their lower nature, possess an active strength which automatically transforms those who fall within their orbit. A commonality of spirit exists in those spiritual experiences. Asceticism and *sādhanā* are the means which permit Catholics, Protestants, Hindus, all people of whatever religion, to become like those great benefactors of humanity.

The word "askesis" or asceticism, taken in its etymological sense, signifies spiritual practice, application, exercise.

The word ''sādhana,'' or discipline, signifies realization, the means employed to obtain an end. The work ''askesis'' has taken on a more restricted sense than *sādhanā*. It is restricted not just to spiritual practice but to that practice associated with the life of monks or others who live in monasteries. The word *sādhanā* has a wider sense. It implies all the ways by which one improves oneself.

The end is the same, but the mortification of Christian askesis is only the final step of *sādhanā*.

There is another difference: *sādhanā* must lead to the realization of happiness, and consequently to a transformation integral to being on this very earth, before the body falls: "He who is able to withstand the force of lust and anger, even here, before he quits the body—he is established in yoga, he is a happy man." (B. G. V: 23). In Christian thought, the highest state one can attain consists in betrothal and spiritual marriage, but beatification is not in this world. An analogous position is found in Hindu theology. The *Gītā*, which constitutes the essence of our philosophical and religious education, gives the assurance that here on earth we can control our animal nature and realize that ascension which leads to God.

One certain fact is this: If we remain where we are, we cannot progress. The burden of our memories is too heavy and prevents us from evolving. Moreover, the state which we wish to realize is veiled by our present state. It is only by forgetting acquired tendencies, our *saṁskāras* or past impressions, that we begin our journey towards evolution. "Intelligent thinking is skillful forgetting," says an old English proverb. St. John of the Cross expresses the same idea in a psychological fashion in his *Ascent of Mount Carmel:* "A form cannot be introduced into a subject if it has not first of all expelled the contrary form; for the latter, so long as it lasts, is an obstacle; there is incompatibility between the two" (*AMC*, Bk I, Ch. VI, 2). There is indeed incompatibility between our animal nature and our divine nature. We have to drive out the inferior animal forms; only then can we advance to a superior level.

So long as a caterpillar thinks it is a caterpillar, it will never become a butterfly. So long as we remain hypnotised by our sinful state and enveloped in our memories, there will be no evolution.

In order to forget our state of sin, we must have certitude. We must be very sure of the possibility of attaining that supreme state where only *ānanda* (bliss) remains. "So long as the soul remains the subject of the senses," says St. John of the Cross, "it is incapable of receiving the purely spiritual."

Faith is what causes the soul, at first folded up within itself, to emerge and little by little open itself to God and live like the saints. That superior state exists, in fact. God is incarnated in order to come and live on earth. In order to have the desire to realize ourselves and forget our primitive nature, we must turn our face towards those beings who are near us and possess the magic power to transform us. Chaitanya* could convert bandits by his mere presence, and Jesus transformed sinners into saints.

Let us keep before ourselves the possibility of our own ascension while never ceasing to affirm the presence of those great Beings. That will be the germ of our asceticism, the beginning of our spiritual discipline.

Looking at ourselves in the indecision and spiritual anxiety of our sinful state, we will never be able to conceive the supreme Being, for "all the being of creatures compared to the Infinite Being of God is only vanity," as St. John of the Cross says in his *Ascent of Mount Carmel.* "What is not has no relation to that which is" (I, 1, 3).

We must break with the past and with special habits of thinking. That is the beginning of the renunciation of self. If we do not detach ourselves from our propensity for all natural goods we can own, there will never be room in us to implant pure divine nature. An infinite distance exists between the particular riches man can possess and the nature of God. "Whoever does not bear his own Cross and come after Me, cannot be my disciple," says Jesus (Luke 14:27).

Faith is what sustains the ascetic: it is what makes the old man in us die and makes our lives fruitful. ". . . unless a grain of wheat falls into the earth and dies, it remains alone; but if it dies, it bears much fruit" (John 12:24). It is voluntary death, which St. John of the Cross calls "night," and we have seen that it is the work of Faith. In this sense Faith, by its transforming virtue, is already Grace. In the *Gītā* it is said that, "Some look on the Self as wonder; some speak of It as a wonder; some hear of It as a wonder; still others, though hearing, do not understand It at all" (II, 29).

We find in the *Padyāvalī* (Vaishnavite verse) that Faith is a unique recompense which millions of existences cannot obtain. That Faith involves a real detachment of the soul, and we have images analogous to those of St. John of the Cross when he speaks of the "Night." "When he completely withdraws the senses from their objects, as a tortoise draws in its limbs, then his wisdom is firmly fixed" (*BG,* II, 58).

He remains in the Self, says the *Gītā* (II, 58). The soul, detached from all its natural tendencies, presents itself to God, stripped of all its natural acquisitions. The soul must stand stark naked before Him. It is the same nakedness one finds in Hindu myths. In the *Bhāgavata Purāṇa** the young Lord Kṛṣṇa steals the clothes of the milk-maids while they are bathing. In the act of complete submission by which they present themselves naked before him, they draw on themselves the blessing of the Lord.

According to the devotional school of Hindu thought, there exists only one masculine being, the Puruṣa, the Supreme Lord, and everything manifested belongs to that whirlwind of matter called *Prakṛti.** So long as our souls remain veiled by the stain of matter we cannot conceive of the refulgence of the Beloved. We must remove the garments of sensual life and put on those of the spirit.

The formula of asceticism, like that of *sādhanā* in its last stages, is indeed that which St. Teresa used to give in her Carmel of Avila. "Solo Dios Basta"—"God alone, and that is enough."

But how can we arrive at that spiritual evolution? How can we submit to that total renunciation?

2. LOVE

In the thought of St. John of the Cross, as in Hindu spirituality, Love holds a very important place: "All becomes insipid where Love does not exist," Brother Lawrence of the Resurrection used to say. Thanks to Love, on the other hand the smallest thing takes on luminous significance.

In the course of asceticism, it is love which makes us overcome the terrible obstacle of dryness. We must thus find it at all costs. For that, starting out aware of our own state of weakness, we must lift up our eyes and gaze steadfastly at the lives of the great saints who were, like us, subject to the laws of matter and imprisoned in a body of flesh. For Christians, Christ represents the perfect image. He is the only Son whom all men should strive to emulate. We have the Buddha, and nearer to our time, Ramakrishna, whose boldness we can admire. As soon as they have found the Supreme Being they leave their fleshly body. Thereby they show us how one practices *sādhanā.*

"Look at the boldness of a Buddha," Swami Brahmananda often would say to us. "In order to realize God he abandoned all comforts of his royal mansion and gave himself up to the most severe austerities. But seeing that he could not get anywhere that way, he sat on the bank of a river and swore thus: 'May this body abandon me, but I will not rise henceforth until I have achieved realization.' And illumination came!" We must live in the company of holy saints and imitate their nature. They alone will be able to teach us the true nature of love, for they have God in them, and God is love itself. "Fire is latent in all things," Sri Ramakrishna would say, "but it manifests itself in a higher degree in wood. God also is present in all things, but He is manifested with much more strength in the saints."

God reveals Himself to us by the intermediary of the Saints. It is in them that we come into personal contact with His grace. Without that encounter on the human level, we would never understand the plenitude and the taste of His love. It is said in the *Nārada Bhakti Sūtras** that though the inclination and the taste for a superior life can be the endowment coming from the spiritual exercises accomplished in the course of a past life, a stimulant coming from the outside is, nevertheless, almost always necessary if its dormant tendencies are to be awakened. For many people, that spiritual awakening is produced only as a result of meeting a perfect soul, a guru. The guru is the inspirer: it is he that brings that spiritual stimulation which even the Incarnations and the Prophets need for the awakening. The guru is the Great Soul to whom we owe our spiritual renewal; his example alone suffices to make us understand that we must be born again.

"The society of the saints leads to devotion through Faith," says the *Bhaktirasāyana*. By living in the company of a Living Incarnation from Scripture, even a man inclined to doubt may succeed in believing in the possibility of realization.

In fact, Love is innate; we do not acquire it. The company of the saints merely reveals it; for having only the Lord in their hearts, they are "the supreme indescribable form of Love (*anirvacanīya prema svarūpa*)." By their means the Lord discloses Himself. It is then that we truly begin our *sādhanā* or spiritual discipline.

Many will say, "But I feel no life; I feel only the contradictions facing me." What they do not wish to see is the existence of the Āt*man* which sustains them. They life from the Absolute Itself, which is the Being of whom they are made and who sustains all the contradictions on which this universe rests. It is in Him that they live and move and have their being. Love is the corollary on the affective level. Love expresses that fundamental identity of all beings who are expressions of the same "Him." That is why, without love, all asceticism or discipline is sterile. Love is the only factor which permits us to make progress on that way.

> Henceforth I will no longer tend my sheep. My only work will be to love. (*SC* XXVIII)

Love creates a resemblance between the lover and the one he loves. It is love which will transform us into the image of the Beloved. Such is the great principle of Christian asceticism; such also is that on which Hindu spirituality rests:

> The turbulent senses, O son of Kunti, violently carry off the mind even of a wise man striving for perfection. When a man dwells on objects, he feels an attachment for them. Attachment gives rise to desire, and desire breeds anger. From anger comes delusion; from delusion, the failure of memory, the ruin of discrimination; and from the ruin of discrimination the man perishes. (*BG*, II, 60-63)

Thus speaks the blessed Lord of the *Gītā*, and he adds: "When a man casts far away from him, Pārtha, all his mind's desire, and when he finds satisfaction in the Self alone, by the Self, that man will have a well-established intelligence" (*BG* II, 55). Of the state which the Sage then attains the *Gītā* speaks in these terms:

> The self-controlled man is awake when it is night for all others. When other men are awake, it is night for the realized sage. (*BG*, II, 69)

These words of the Blessed Lord seem to be taken up by St. John of the Cross when he writes in his poem:

> On a dark night,
> Starving for love and deep in flame,
> O happy lucky flight!
> Unseen I slipped away,
> My house at last was calm and safe.
>
> On that happy night—in Secret;
> No one saw me through the dark—

And I saw nothing then,
No other light to mark
The way but fire pounding in my heart.

O night, my guide!
O night more friendly than the dawn!
O tender night that tied
Lover and the loved one,
Loved one in the lover fused as one! (*AMC*, Stanzas 1, 3, 5)

You can see how these two texts give great importance to detachment, to individual asceticism.

The best of our interior cultures, *The Secret Road which Leads to the Divine,* is described in the same way. Whether it is a question of Hindu or Christian sensitivity, the first step to take consists of detaching ourselves from everything which, up to now, has been represented as the veritable reality: the world of the senses and the intellect for which we were living. Painful birth into that light! The soul abandons one by one the garments which adorned her in order to go, alone and naked, in a direction which she has never explored, unaccompanied by any familiar notions. Leaving the shores where she seemed to find a light, she goes towards the unknown, guided only by faith. Love in the soul, however dim, suffices to illuminate unawares. Love in the Beloved necessarily rivals whatever it gives to the things of the earth.

That night of senses, that night of intelligence, and that night of spirituality, is worth the pain of passing through, for they precede the light of the Day. To use the language of St. John of the Cross, "O blessed night, my guide! O night more friendly than the dawn!"

That tenebrous pre-dawn light in which the Carmelite ascetic journeys is the prelude to the dazzling daybreak of the Hindu *Bhakta.* Bursting forth into the full day, we bless the ark which carried us through obscurity and incertitude. For "Where all beings are awake, there is night for the sage who sees."

3. REVELATION

Let us now see how askesis and *sādhanā* are justified by Revelation. Man, such as he is, is incapable of discovering by himself the light which will illuminate him in the dark. His emotions, like his intelligence, are naturally impure and veiled. Revelation comes to help him discover the way, showing him the path of purification.

The manner in which we consider Revelation, however, is different in our two civilizations. With us, Revelation is atemporal, is not an event born in time. It is the primordial sound, the *śabda* Brahman heard by the sages, vibrating eternally.

We consider it as the supreme Knowledge, the Veda which human intelligence will not be able to surpass or even equal. Not being irrational but "transrational," it is what illuminates human intelligence and brings to it the plenitude it was lacking.

With Christians, on the contrary, Revelation is temporal: it is a dialogue between man and divinity. Divine interventions correspond to the needs of man concerning his earthly establishment and his destiny. God appears above all as the chief of a people to whom He communicates something of His authority. His presence among his people is revealed by the Law.

That Law, however, is not complete. It is a promise; its realization must await the appearance of the Son. The Son is the completed Word. I let St. John of the Cross speak.

> Formerly it was necessary to ask God regarding matters of the Faith and they were revealed in response to the questions of men. With Christ, who is the complete word, God has given us everything. He has nothing more to give us... What God has revealed to our Fathers in various times and various ways in former times, he has spoken in these last days, finally and all at once, through his Son." (*AMC*, Bk II, Ch. 22, 3, 4)

We have only to look to the Son, the paradigm of eternal Wisdom. St. Paul also affirms, "in whom [Christ] are hid all the treasures of wisdom and knowledge" (Col. 2:3).

Thus it is in the Son that all Wisdom henceforth resides. He is, according to the very words of God, as they are understood by St. John of the Cross, *all my word, all my revelation.*

God has nothing more to reveal to us. To ask something further from Him would be to wrong Him:

> If someone came to question me, as they used to do, and ask me for some kind of vision or revelation, it is, in a way, asking me for Christ or asking me for more faith than I have

> given: so he would profoundly offend my Beloved Son, because not only would he show thereby that he had no faith in Him, but he would further oblige Him to become incarnate again, to begin his life over, and die once more. (*AMC*, Bk. II, Ch. 22,5)

It is thus that St. John of the Cross has God speak; thus for a Christian, Christ represents the Supreme Wisdom. St. John of the Cross quotes St. Paul:

> For I decided to know nothing among you except Jesus Christ and him crucified. (I Cor, 2:2)

St. John of the Cross adds:

> If you wish still other visions or divine revelations, look again into humanity. You will find much more than you expect (*AMC*, Bk. II, 22, 4). For in him lives bodily the plenitude of divinity. (Col. 2:9)

Such is the just doctrine: it is by Christ made man, according to his Church and his ministers, that we are to be guided. It is there that we will find the remedies for our spiritual weakness and abundant aid for all our needs. One must believe nothing of anything which comes from elsewhere. "But even if we, or an angel from heaven, should preach to you a gospel contrary to that which we preached to you, let him be accursed" (Gal. 1:8). And St. John of the Cross adds: "We must always hold to what Christ taught us; the rest is nothing; and we must not believe what does not conform to his teaching" (*ibid*, p. 7).

Such is the essence of Christian thought. We must, in order to understand it, set aside our prejudices. I warn admirers of Hindu thought against the temptation to see this way of thinking as narrow and intransigent. To judge the Christian viewpoint in that way would be to lack tolerance, for that would prove our incapacity to adopt temporarily a viewpoint different from the one we admire. In the name of Hindu thought, which has tolerance as a basic tenet, I ask you to find the angle of vision and adopt the perspective which is that of St. John of the Cross. You will then understand that, *given the premises laid down by the Old Testament*, the Christian way of thinking is the only one which can be rigorous, the only one which can be true. What appears to an outsider as intransigence is, from the Christian point of view, a necessity if he is to live spiritually. *There cannot be for a Catholic Christian any other way of understanding.* To ask Christians to adopt a different point of view or to admit a broader perspective in the name of tolerance is to show oneself to be very intolerant. For new ideas break the proper line of their development; they sow trouble and break the harmony of the edifice which tradition patiently built up, choosing each of the stones from revelation and crowning the whole with the spire of faith in our Lord Jesus Christ.

Those who would try, under the mask of a sterile syncretism, to introduce philosophic ideas foreign to the accepted bases of theology as St. John of the Cross interprets it, could rightly be considered as "demoniacal influences" who sow perturbation in souls who possess the precious gift of faith.

The man who wishes to remain loyal to his faith cannot hold to a dogma while offering allegiance to a foreign dogma. The risk he would run in that case would be to fashion a mixture of traditions, generate confusion, and make for a shallow culture. Such a mixture of traditions is one of the signs of a degradation which characterizes our *Kali-Yuga.**

In undertaking this series of lectures, my intention is not to insist on dogmas and doctrines but on the transformation which can enrich the inner man. Seen from that point of view, Hindu, Christian, or Muslim doctrines reveal the same power of transformation. We consider them as the autonomous steps in the expression of the genius of each people in their search for God.

We do not ask Christians to accept our position; we simply invite them, when studying a foreign dogma, to adopt the viewpoint appropriate to that new tradition. It is by taking that position that the alleged intransigence of the Christian position will become then in our eyes the very characteristic of that position.

In giving this series of lectures, I have no intention of minimizing the scope of Christian thought by comparing it with our thought. In St. John of the Cross we find ourselves before a mystic of the first order, destined to be considered by all religions of the world as a true saint, one who belongs to all traditions. It is said of the poet and saint Kabir that after his death the Hindu divinities and the Muslim angels met to argue over his body. In reading St. John of the Cross I, although a Hindu monk, can offer the same veneration as we offer our greatest ascetics.

This brief study enables us to see that spiritual life is presented differently in the two traditions. In the two traditions spiritual life has neither the same perspective nor the same foundation.

With us, there is an extra-temporal revelation, unrelated to human history (*apauruṣeya*). It is the integral Knowledge, the Brahman-sound (*Śabda*-Brahman), which does not cease to resonate, designating for human wisdom several equally valid means for reaching that "which, being known, makes known to all the rest" (*Muṇḍaka Upaniṣad* I.1.3). Among Christians we find, on the contrary, a strictly temporal revelation involving a certain history or section of humanity and culminating in a person who bears in himself all wisdom and whose merit extends at the same time over all the future and all the past. The difference in the framework of spiritual life is translated into askesis and *sādhanā*.

For the Christian, Christ becomes the model, the way, the life. "One must desire to imitate Christ in all things," says St. John of the Cross (*AMC*, Bk. I, Ch. 13, 3). For that, it is necessary to contemplate his life in such a way as to act in everything as he would have done. That is the great principle of askesis:

> If your senses are offered some pleasure which is not purely for the honour and glory of God, it is necessary to mortify yourself and renounce, out of love for Jesus Christ, who never had during his life on earth any other desire than to do the will of his Father; this he called his food and sustenance. (*Ibid.*, 4)

Thus St. John of the Cross expresses himself as he describes the road souls must take in order to enter into the night. Thence arises the tendency to consider the spiritual life as identical with mortification. The way Christ preaches in the Sermon on the Mount is indeed an ascetic way:

> He who does not take his cross and follow me is not worthy of me. He who finds his life will lose it, and he who loses his life for my sake will find it. (Matt. 10:38-39)

Such is the monastic way, the way of the Beatitudes, reserved for rare souls, the elect.

In India, such teachings are not presented to a multitude. Renunciation is taught to a qualified disciple. It is a *rahasya* (secret), an esoteric teaching. Aspirants are rare. The ideal of *ahiṁsā*, such as it is described in our Scriptures, "without hate for any being, friendly and compassionate, etc." (*BG* XII, 13) is the ideal of the Sage. It cannot be that of everyone, for *ahiṁsā* implies not only abstention from outward aggression but from all evil thoughts which are bearers of violence. This high ideal is that of men who have already passed through the stages of *tamas** and *rajas**. It belongs to those whose spirit is *sāttvik*,* pure and liberated. To wish to follow, cost what may, the way of integral mortification, which we call *nivṛtti mārga*,* arouses great distress in oneself. Many people wonder how one can practice Christ's message in our century. It can be done only by complete renunciation.

4. DHARMA*

What, then, becomes of the others, those not yet ready to renounce? *Sādhanā* offers them a positive way, that of *pravṛtti mārga*. It is the way of action. Before renouncing one's self, one must develop it.

We are at present in a formative state. Several islets of *saṁskāras*, whirling and disparate centres, dispute the direction of our personality; and we float then randomly like a rubber ball on the waves. In developing our personality in a given direction, by practicing the proper *dharma* (*svadharma*), our active will, becoming enlightened, develops our personality on the level of *rajas* (activity). Right action transforms our primitive dispersion into a living, ordered unity.

When this *rajas* itself is purified by practicing the virtues, the soul, a ripe unblemished fruit, is ready to fall at the feet of the Divine, like a steel ball which drops to the ocean floor. Before thinking of total abnegation, it is necessary to acquire a certain density in our character. We achieve it by observing the science of *dharma* (*Dharmaśàstra*).

We cite here two verses of the *Gītā* which will clarify our thought:

> Exceedingly dear to Me are they who regard Me as the Supreme Goal, and endowed with faith and devotion, follow this Immortal Dharma. (XII, 20)

> Therefore let the Scriptures be your authority in determining what ought to be done and what ought not to be done. Having learned the injunctions of scriptures, you should work in the world. (XVI, 24)

In order to dissolve into universal life, one must have previously passed through all degrees.

Sādhanā begins with infancy, as soon as the parents and later the spiritual instructor initiate the child into universal order. The contemplation of the cosmos to which his prayers accustom him (prayers to Varuṇa, Mitra, Vāyu, Bṛhaspati—the sky, the sun, the ether and all great cosmic forces) expands his spirit in the direction of the universal. The idea of the harmony of all (*ṛta**) absorbs the idea of his particular individuality. Like a drop of dew in the morning sun, his egoism melts into universal life. The advantage of primitive societies is that they do not interpose between man and the universe a veil of artificial notions, products of mechanized civilizations. Primitive man possesses a mentality which is open and pulsating with the very rhythm of things. The child becomes accustomed to saluting the beings to whom he owes his life: The *Devas,** the *Pitṛs,** the *Ṛṣis;** and he offers them sacrifices. For, "those who enjoy the objects given by the Devas without giving them anything in return are thieves" (*BG* III, 12). It is thus that he learns his *Dharma.* The great events which occur later, such as marriage, births, etc., are occasions once again to get in touch with that divine harmony. (You can find the nuptial ceremony described in the *Bṛhadāraṇyaka Upaniṣad* VI, 4). The act of procreation is considered a cosmic sacrifice.

Such is the first stage of *sādhanā,* the awakening of the spirit to the meaning of the law (*Dharma*). One becomes conscious of the position which he occupies in the world and establishes himself in harmony with the All.

In the act of oblation which tradition imposes on him, the individual feels awakening in him the spiritual forces which will not cease henceforth to assist his upward course. It is the *dharmasādhanā.* It is the way for men of the world, those who live in the *gṛhasthāśramas*—the family hearth. From there, the movement towards the *saṁnyāsa-āśrama,* the monastic discipline, normally occurs. Then he arrives at the practice of *Mokṣa-sādhanā,* categorical renunciation.

Dharma, the reflection on our little earth of the great cosmic forces, raises the problem of material goods and their use for our spiritual advancement. We are not yet asked to reject desire. We must find beforehand the *dhārmika* means of satisfying desire.

Man must thus learn to manage material goods, to acquire them and provide for the departed spirits and satisfy the gods. Without material goods there is no sacrifice. It is with them that man honours all powers of heaven. This discipline is called *artha-sādhanā*. *Kāma-sādhanā* is an effort to integrate, on the social level, the natural expression of the pulsation of desires, the expression indispensable for preventing repression. All desires which are in accord with social law, with *dharma*, are approved and sanctified. Other residual desires in the natural animal within us belong to whatever there is of the demonic, the *āsurisampad*: they must be carefully fought off.

In ancient India, there was no place for the profane. All was sacred. Each act of daily life adhered to a cosmic function which it imitated in brief. This interconnection of the material plane with the spiritual, of the gross with the subtle, is affirmed at each moment of the day by rites. The manner in which worldly men live thus quite naturally leads to spirituality. The different *sādhanās* are so many ways which permit the sanctification of human existence and the divinization of life.

Proportionately to the degree of evolution of each particular soul, through the three states of *prakṛti* (*tamas, rajas, sattva*), *sādhanā* accompanies the person's development until he is completely liberated, which he will reach by renunciation, by *Mokṣa-sādhanā*. Before attaining it, the soul begins by giving a legitimate place to the sensory satisfactions and permits a regulated enjoyment of all good things. Hindu thought sees in every effect the richness of the Cause, which is divinity. The end of revelation is to make the ordinary man find God himself at the interior of this sensible world of the senses filled with qualities. The asceticism will come only later, once the great moral virtues have been implanted; discrimination having been awakened, the aspirant will begin himself to renounce this world and other worlds, in his more and more ardent thirst for liberation. The ascetic is born when the aspirant discovers the negative character of the content of empirical reality.

As St. John of the Cross says: "Passion, agreeable to the palate at first, becomes bitter to the stomach. It won't take long for the soul to feel its bitterness and its sad effects" (*AMC*, Bk. I, Ch. 12, 5). We find the same idea in the *Gītā*, XVIII, 38.

Experience teaches man that if he runs after the limited things of this world, he harvests only dissatisfaction and vanity. "A soul scattered among frivolous objects is like water which, once poured out, cannot be picked up," says St. John of the Cross.

It is thus by the way of asceticism or poverty that one will henceforth seek plenitude.

Sādhanā thus rejects nothing of this world. It does not consider that an abyss exists between it and God. An abyss impossible to fill. *Sādhanā* strives to see that abyss with eyes which spiritualize it and transcend limits.

> The Lord said: 'Even of yore, O sinless one, a twofold devotion was taught by me to the world: devotion to knowledge for the contemplative and devotion to work for the active.' (*BG* III, 3)

It is simply necessary to know what we are in order to choose between the two. In any case, there will be an ascension towards askesis, which is the renunciation of self. Life is not congealed. It does not cease to develop according to the laws which are proper to it, and we must complete the stages of purification before mounting towards the Supreme. Nothing would be served by wishing to hasten that ascension. One's proper *Dharma* even badly used is worth more than the *Dharma* of another even if properly used. The faith of each depends on his particular aptitude (*BG*).

Thus spiritual aspirants climb upwards. The twice-born represent the final degree of evolution: they "Honour purity, uprightness, and the absence of aggressiveness." They are men "honest in their intent, full of serenity of spirit, who have the privilege of goodness and silence" (*ibid.*).

Before being an ethic of deliverance, an askesis or a *Sādhanā* is a temporal ethic which leads the soul by the way of transmigrations through more and more elevated states of existence. In the course of this advance towards liberation, the soul becomes more and more luminous, because it becomes more and more pure. In its final state of perfect purity, if becomes the friend of all creation.

> With the heart concentrated by yoga, viewing all things with equal regard, he beholds himself in all beings and all beings in himself. (*BG* VI, 29)

Such is the description the blessed Kṛṣṇa gives of the man who has accomplished all stages of perfect purification and who, having passed by the way of askesis, has become the Siddha, the perfect one.

It is the secret stairway of St. John of the Cross by which the soul, having escaped during the night from the corporeal prison, sets out for her meeting with the Beloved.

3

The Study of Yoga in Saint John of the Cross

1. Preliminary Considerations Concerning Spiritual Studies[1]

As a preface to this third lecture on comparative mysticism, I will begin by some cautionary advice: "My principal intention," St. John of the Cross wrote, "is not to address myself to everyone in general but rather to a few people, to members of the Reform of Our Lady of Mount Carmel" (*AMC*, Bk I, prologue, 9).

Laymen feel more and more inclined to read works written for monks, and the temptation for them is great, under the pretext of following a way full of prestige, to lose their stability and to stray from the law of their own *Dharma*. That happens when heads of families, the *Gṛhasthas* in India, read books such as *Monastic Discipline*, discourses of Swami Brahmananda.* The Swami was not addressing all monks, for most of us are given to an active life oriented towards the ideal of Vivekananda: service to men and help for the needy. When Swami Brahmananda advises consecrating

---

[1]This lecture was delivered at the Sorbonne on March 19, 1949 under the title, "Etude du Yoga chez Saint Jean de la Croix."

the whole day to meditation, not sleeping more than three or four hours, and not filling more than two-thirds of the stomach, he is speaking to monks living far from the centres of action, in the cells of monasteries in Benares or the Himalayas; they are the monks who practice austerities, the discipline of mortification.

A man of the world who undertakes monastic disciplines without precautions, who, fascinated by the novelty of that extraordinary life, tries to live at that pitch, risks losing his equilibrium. His mind, divided between contrary notions, oscillates between attitudes so opposed to one another that he could very well lose forever his centre of gravity. The confusion of values is one of the signs which characterizes the degradation of our era, this *Kali-Yuga*, which, according to Indian mythology, was to be the *Yuga* at the end of time. Rare indeed are those who still read the Śāstras (Scriptures), those treatises of ancient wisdom which prescribe progressive stages of existence through which the aspirant must pass before attaining the full renunciation of *Saṁnyāsa*.

Meditating at night is not an exercise to be undertaken by the head of the family. It is suitable only for those who have accepted to live close to death.

Disciplines advised by monks are disciplines which, followed without compromises, permit, according to the words of St. Teresa of Avila, "Taking the citadel of God by storm." When I visited the monks of the monastery of the Grande Chartreuse, I was given copies of a picture on which they meditated there. It is the face of a skeleton dressed in the robe of a monk. In seeing it you would be seized by terror.

Despite the warnings given and the precautions taken, we in India are responsible for the confusion created by our publications. When spiritual anguish, always latent in people, encounters the appeasement of the word of God, they seize the occasion thus offered, and then search desperately to put into practice in all its details teachings which were not intended for them. This is extremely dangerous. "If, in order to get more quickly to the roof of a house, you try to jump up instead of slowly climbing the stairs," Swami Brahmananda told us, "you risk breaking your neck."

That is what laymen do when, without preparation, they try to put into practice the teachings of St. John of the Cross. To wish, while in the world, to know the "Dark Night" and attain liberation, is to succumb to a spirit of competition and ambition which brings in its train only confusion and suffering. The hierarchical life which we follow in India when it is a matter of *Sādhanā* does not allow this confusion of levels. The Disciplines valid for a *Saṁnyāsin* are not suitable for a *Gṛhastha*, and whoever, notwithstanding the prohibition's social wisdom, would try to conform to them, would be doing so in full consciousness of derogating the laws of his *Dharma*. A true Guru would then invite him to reintegrate his way.

Aspirants leading a family life are rarely suited to the ascetic life. In ancient times, that category of *Gṛhasthas* formed the class of the *Vānaprastha*. That stage has disappeared. Ramakrishna counsels worldly aspirants to live as brother and sister in marriage after having had two or three children. When discipline is thus introduced into sex life, other rules concerning meditation and eating follow automatically. Hindu thought, moreover, here in agreement with Christian doctrine, considers the encounter with God possible at any stage of life. Knowledge of God is fortunately not subject to laws of causality. It depends only on grace, which knows no law.

However, the elimination of worldly activities, so necessary for the infusion of the Divine Presence, can be done only gradually. After the individual has passed through the earlier stages of family life, professional life, etc., he can disengage himself from inferior attachments and begin a mortification more and more complete, until he attains finally the summit in *Saṁnyāsa āśrama*. Christ taught everyone virtues which can only be practiced by monks:

> Do not lay up for yourselves treasures on earth, where moth and rust consume . . . but lay up for yourselves treasures in heaven. (Matthew 6:19-21)
>
> You have heard that it was said, 'an eye for an eye and a tooth for a tooth.' But I say unto you, 'Do not resist one who is evil. But if anyone strikes you on the right cheek, turn to him the other also; and if any one would sue you and take your coat, let him have your cloak as well.' (Matthew 5:38-40)
>
> Therefore I tell you, do not be anxious about your life, what you shall eat or what you shall drink, nor about your body, what you shall put on . . . Look at the birds of the air; they neither sow nor reap nor gather into barns, and yet your heavenly Father feeds them. Are you not of more value

> than they? And which of you being anxious can add one cubit to his span of life? And why are you anxious about clothing? Consider the lilies of the field, how they grow; they neither toil nor spin; yet I tell you even Solomon in all his glory was not arrayed like one of these . . . Therefore do not be anxious, saying, 'What shall we eat? What shall we wear?' For the Gentiles seek all these things; and your heavenly Father knows that you need them all. But seek first his kingdom and his righteousness, and all these things shall be yours as well. (Matthew 6:25-33)

This absolute renunciation is characteristic of the *Paramahaṁsa*, that is to say of the *Saṁnyāsin* of the highest order. Sri Ramakrishna used to say that the soul which has attained that degree of evolution abandons herself completely to the divine will, like a leaf blown by the wind. He would compare also that eminently monastic attitude to that of a man who lets go of a high tree and lets himself fall without trying to catch hold of a branch:

> The state of abandoning yourself to God is that state of complete relaxation which the tired labourer feels when, after a day of work, he leans back on a pillow for a leisurely smoke. It's the end of anxiety and care. All that which remains to be done will be done by Him. (*Gospel*, p. 209)

Thus live the *Mukta-Puruṣa*, the liberated ones, without egotism or self-will. They go where God impels them, without remembering the past or making plans for the future.

Only a very few monks can realize that state. The whole earth is their home, and the sky is their roof. Although Jesus addressed the crowd, the discipline of renunciation and the practice of unconcern cannot become from one day to the next the prerogative of everyone. Those virtues are incompatible with the atmosphere of family life. It is in the teachings of St. Paul, as of Manu in our country, that we find a conciliation. Although the teaching of Christ is a teaching essentially monastic, uncompromising ("no man can serve two masters, for either he will hate one and love the other, or he will become attached to one and will despise the other. You cannot serve God and Mammon" [Luke 13:16])—this teaching is for us that of *Mokṣha-Sādhanā*, of liberation—society has nevertheless tried somehow to adopt it in order to be

"Christian." But we must not forget that in this adaptation of the Sermon on the Mount to the world something has been lost of its intransigence and its ascetic purity.

Truth, in a mind pure and stripped of worldly attachments, is reflected in its entirety. But in a mind troubled and burdened by preoccupations of a material nature, truth is reflected with difficulty, and its reflection seems distorted. It seems, so to speak, to adapt itself to obstacles which it meets on the surface of the mirror. The truth is still there, but truncated and partial. Each region of the manifestation—*Tamas, Rajas, Sattva**—takes what it can, whatever corresponds to the degree of evaluation of the soul within *Prakṛti.*

The confusion which some people experience after reading such works such as those of St. John of the Cross has its source in a disregard for that law of evolution and the existence of different *aśramas* (stages). For each state a precise *Sādhanā* is applied which one must respect if one wants to continue to develop in a balanced way.

> It is better for each person to do his duty even
> imperfectly than to do someone else's however well.
> It is better to perish following one's own law;
> It is perilous to follow the law of another. (*BG*, XVIII, 47)

But why have I chosen to speak of St. John of the Cross? That saint is indeed a prince among monks, and we are worldly people who have family obligations and a social *Dharma* to observe.

In the teaching of the saint, besides the disciplines intended exclusively for monks, something universally valid exists which is beneficial for us. I wish to meet the personality still vibrant behind these pages, a meeting with the saint. One finds the same thing reading *Monastic Disciplines.* Swami Brahmanda is before you and you are, without suspecting it, impregnated by the radiance of his personality. The spirituality of these men is a power still at work in the world. That spirituality invades us as we turn those pages which transform us unawares and gives us new peace. We breathe for a while in the atmosphere of those men who attained the highest summits of humanity. Four centuries have passed and the conviction of the Spanish saint can still be felt:

> My beloved is like the mountains,
> Like the solitary wooded valleys . . .

He is like the tranquil night
When dawn begins to rise,
Like silent music, like harmonious solitude,
Like the banquet which delights and fills with love. (*SC*: 14, 15)

Romain Rolland,* speaking of Swami Vivekananda, notes with astonishment, "Despite the distance which separates us, we feel when we open his books such an animated presence, that it seems as though his fiery breath falls directly on us and rouses us to action."

When I read St. John of the Cross myself, I am often carried away by the radiance of his person. It is not so much the content of his thought which grasps me, as the blessedness I feel emanating from such holy company.

I have had the privilege of breathing the atmosphere of certain great souls. Then it was not so much the content of their teaching which attracted me. That was only an almost trifling emanation of their character. There was something ennobling about them which cannot be communicated in words. It is that very presence we find in their works which is communicated to posterity.

This radiance is not the monopoly of monks: it exists around the great sages who are the glory of humanity. I have undertaken this series of lectures to invite you to come and share that feeling. The greatest part of the teaching of the saint is for monks, but his person is for everyone.

In this day and age, when all spiritual values are on trial, we need the presence of a saint living among us and interpreting for us the sense of our destiny. In following what we can use of his word, we inaugurate in ourselves a new personality: from an animal state we raise ourselves to the reasonable state; our human life draws near the angelic life, and from the temporal and human that we were, we become celestial and divine. St. John of the Cross, in fact, taking up the words of St. Paul, characterizes the sensual man as an "animal who understands nothing of the things of God" (*AMC*, Bk. III, Ch. 26, 4); whereas he who turns his affections towards God he calls, after the words of St. Paul, "a spiritual man who penetrates and judges everything, even the deep things of God" (I Cor. 2:10, 14).

We can all hope for this kind of transformation for ourselves.

To have pure thoughts, to be charitable, to master our wrath—it is there that the saints aid us. This salutary transformation which is brought about by great personalities is sufficient to give us faith. In the presence of St. John of the Cross, it is not necessary to "believe": "Faith is communicated to us with subtlety." For a Ramakrishna, a Ramaṇa Maharṣhi,* a Swami Ramdas, teaching is not needed. It is enough to live near them, and their spirituality invades us.

It was after reading St. Teresa of the Child Jesus that a friend of mine, now a member of the order of Discalced Carmelites, left everything for the service of God. The preternatural touched him unawares; faith was given to him. The great lay disciple of Ramakrishna, the author of the *Kathāmṛta*, who signed his name "M,"* replied one day to someone who asked him what he had learned in the company of the Master: "I learned nothing: all was communicated to us directly. A breath fell upon us and we were awakened. In the same way, we can be directly touched upon by the works coming from a liberated soul."

Do not distress yourself if you do not succeed right away in practicing teachings of the Saints. Let us be content to take from their lives what matters, that is, the aspect of faith. It is that which will give us the assurance of our coming liberation and the resurrection of the future man.

2. ASPECTS OF *JÑĀNA YOGA* IN ST. JOHN OF THE CROSS

As the title for this lecture, I have chosen the study of *yoga* in St. John of the Cross. The term *yoga*, although exotic, can be used to characterize the thought of the saint. Not because it is a term which enjoys great popularity just now, but because it indicates that union with God which St. John of the Cross succeeded in living. You are familiar with the four branches of *Yoga*: *Jñāna*, union by knowledge; *Bhakti*, union through love; *Karma*, union through action; and *Rāja*, which consists of a physical and mental discipline which integrates the other three.

I want to present to you St. John of the Cross the way the Hindu sees him. Let us try to study the thought of the Saint in a kind of spiritual spectroscope and see the rays which are absorbed by his own thought. Ordinarily, one considers St. John of the Cross to be a *Jñānin.* In 1937, on the cover of *'Etudes Carmélitaines,'* the portrait of St. John of the Cross appeared side by side with a portrait of our great *Jñāna* sage, Ramaṇa Maharṣhi. But is the thought of the Saint really pure *Jñāna*? It seems to me impossible to say.

Jñāna is pure knowledge, that of the One without a second. It does not imply a religious attitude, for it excludes *a priori* (reasoning from cause to effect) all notions belonging to the world of existence and value. A *jñānin* is indifferent to the matter that whatever lives might follow the present life. He tries to see things from another angle, not that of the spectator interested in a certain zone of existence, but under that of the spectator himself. The *jñānin* mounts again and again towards Being; he does not remain in any of the *étants* (to use existential terminology). All the *étants*' vision of God, hearing of His Words, even beatification, are only *étants,* that is to say, projections by which Being is manifested, but which are not Him. Thus they are, for the *jñānin,* who has realized Being, only spectacles — *dṛśya* — by appearance of which he ceases to be affected, since he participates in true nature, that unique Being in which he is stabilized. The true *jñānin* is a man of established intelligence.

Ramakrishna recounts a humorous incident in the life of that great Vedāntic ascetic, Tota Puri.* Tota Puri was meditating one day when a *deva* appeared before him. Without being in the least disturbed, Tota Puri continued his meditation. A bit ruffled by his impassive attitude, the newcomer asked, "Don't you know who I am?" and Tota Puri replied, "Who are you?" "I am a divine spirit, a deva." "You are a form of Māyā," calmly concluded Tota Puri. "The *Ātman* in you and in me is the same." On hearing these words the spirit vanished.

"Who knows Brahman becomes the *Ātman* of all beings," says the '*Taittirīya Upaniṣad*',—a man perfectly master of himself. From then on he seeks neither saviour nor redeemer. His position no longer tallies with that of the dualistic schools which consider the person as different from the Absolute Being who created him. The difference here between the Creator and the creature consists only in the *upādhis,* that is to say, the evanescent forms with which the *Ātman* is identified. This attitude of the *jñānin* is not based on a union in the strict sense, for there are not two principles. There is only one which must be discovered. Knowledge is not an acquisition: It is a lifting of veils. Knowledge consists in forgetting the error into which one fell. Until then, one was thinking two and two make five. One perceives one day that they make four. Intelligence is freed. Likewise, one was believing that images of the world were real, that they have consistency and individuality; one perceives abruptly that they are only the appearances of a unique Being, the only real, the only true.

The light supplied by this knowledge transforms not only the intelligence but the personality, bathed then in a new life created by comprehension and love. It is what we call Wisdom, that state of supreme consciousness where there is no possibility of error. Being lives in truth. It is at the centre of all beings, Being itself. What does it lack in order to attain bliss? In the West people often think that to become a *jñānin* it is enough to be dissatisfied with the teachings of a church and to have understood something from reading Vivekananda's '*Jñāna Yoga*' or some studies on Ramaṇa Maharṣhi. *Jñāna* has nothing in common with the play of the intellect. It is a leap of intellect beyond its own frontiers, and that event happens unexpectedly when all the avenues of intellect are acknowledged to be dead ends. Then the Self is revealed. Human possibilities were exhausted, but the mind of the seeker had remained *sāttvik*. It is said in the *Kaṭha Upaniṣad* (II, 23), "The *Ātman* reveals itself to whom it pleases."

Thus it is not sufficient to become refractory to some formal teaching in order to consider oneself a *jñānin*, since for the majority of those who break away from reasons for believing imposed by a church do so only in order to be free to seek other reasons. They remain thus within the rational processes of thought, influenced by a theological formation, whatever the terminology they use, even that of the different schools of materialism. The search for a cause, whatever name be given it, will never open the way to a veritable metaphysics.

For my part, I have never met in Europe anyone gifted with the character of a true *jñānin*. In India, the only person possessing that intransigence, which we admired in Tota Puri, is our great sage Ramaṇa Maharṣhi.*

So it is rare to find a pure *jñānin*; perhaps one might be discovered in the Greek tradition. The *jñānin* is a man who, facing life, rejects the way of opinion, what the Greeks called doxa, and which we call *Puruṣa-Tantra*. What he wants is to seize Being in its purity; that is to say, abandoning all which could be personal in his search—intelligence, with its particular procedures of discovery and effectivity. That pure intuition of reality we call *Vastu Tantra.* The object known here is *Ātman Brahman,* which has as a characteristic of being also the subject which knows.

When it is a question of knowledge through the intellect, there are many ways of looking at it. Consider only the different interpretations which men have been able to find for life after death. Each of those speculations projects on its object the shadow of our affectivity and of our individual ways of thinking. Thereby we hide from ourselves the true nature of the thing (*vastu*) instead of aiding ourselves to discover it.

In consideration of the difficulty humans have in breaking away from their hunger for knowledge (in the sense of "knowing" which consists of letting the natural mechanism of the intellect have free play), God has given us Revelation. There exist several revelations dictating to men different ways of seeing proper to the regulation of their activities here on earth.

The religious attitude is thus entirely different from that of Wisdom.

This first is speculation directed by the law of first and final causes, which depends on the fluctuations of the temperament of the seeker.

The search for the first cause, however, is impossible. The entire universe presents itself as an effect. When we find the cause of a given effect, we find only the anterior condition, which is an effect relative to an antecedent condition which will be found to be equally an effect, and so on to infinity. No one will be able thus to see the First Cause. We will never see anything but effects. The search for cause is an intellectual need. The postulation of a first cause is equally a need. But there is no cause which itself is not caused, that is to say which is not in space and time. All cause is in the domain of *māyā*,* of appearances. Thus it is absurd to say that one can encounter God while remaining in this universe, because one will never encounter anything but effects. "Whoever sees God must die," says the Old Testament, "My face you cannot see, for no man may see me and live" (Yahweh to Moses, Exodus, 33:20).

We, in India, say that the primordial cause is the manifestation of the seminal state; it is *avyakta,* the non-manifested. Those who attain it in *samādhi* no longer come back into the domain of names and forms. They disappear in the unmanifested, and for them it is the end of all transmigration. Only divine incarnations contain in themselves the First Cause and its manifestation at the same time. How can that be done? There is no response to that question: "Although I am not born, am of unchangeable nature and Lord of all beings, nevertheless putting on the yoke of my *Prakṛti*, I take form inside my own *Māyā*," says the Blessed Lord (*BG*, IV, 6).

You can see that Hindu thought is not exempt from mystery, something that I think shocks many of its admirers. It is just because there is no rational explanation here that Hindu thinkers have left the religious plane and arrived at *jñāna*.

The search for the cause, unsatisfactory in itself, does not give absolute knowledge. It remains on the plane of *māyā*. In order to transcend that plane, the aspirant must rid himself progressively of the five envelopes which constitute his empirical personality: that of the body: *annamayakośa*; that of vital Energy: *prāṇamayakośa*; that of the mind: *manomayakośa*; that of intelligence: *vijñānamayakośa*; that of bliss: *ānandamayakośa*.

The *Ātman*,* the sole veritable Being, is hidden behind these envelopes. They are only impermanent veils with which it identifies itself. The *jñānin* lives in that pure consciousness beyond the regions of causality. The names and forms which constitute this empirical world belong then to its perfect consciousness, like dreams by which its mind ceases to be troubled. "For it, there is neither destruction nor creation; no one is imprisoned, no one liberated; there exist neither aspirants for liberation nor liberated beings.

Thus speaks Gauḍapāda* in his '*Kārikā*.' The world is the domain of nescience. Of it one may say: "From a magical grain, a magical sprout is born; that sprout is neither permanent nor perishable. Such are the things and with the same reasons." Brahman is real, the world is a dream: that radical knowledge is given in the radical intuition of the *Ātman*.

Never will the relation of causality accord us that perfect intelligibility, for it is content to bind up what occurs in the domain of phenomenality. Seizing what is behind the appearances, the *jñānin* reaches that which is not unreal—*sat*; what is not unconscious– *cit*; what is not deprived of bliss—*ānanda*.

The world is without cause; it is not real. It belongs to the domain of opinion. The reality, which the *jñānin* apprehends, is of the order of *sat-cit-ānanda*.

Insofar as St. John of the Cross is a seeker of the Supreme Cause, one cannot say of him that he is a pure *jñānin.* For him God remains the Father of creatures, the Supreme Cause to which the world is subordinated. When the soul is united with Him, it remains despite that union, different from the Spirit which illuminates it. Certainly, "The soul is transformed; it participates in that which is God, it appears to be God rather than the soul; it is God by participation [but] it conserves its natural being, as distinct from God as before, despite its transformation, as the window is distinct from the ray which shines through it" (*AMC,* Bk. II, Ch. 5, 7).

It seems that in the *yoga* of St. John of the Cross the notion of Creator and creature still remains. The union with God, for him, is realization by faith.

Because of that, you can understand why we say that the saint is not a metaphysical *jñānin.* For pure *jñāna,* the search itself is a myth. It postulates a structure of the intellect incompatible with the metaphysical position of pure Being.

We find, however, in St. John of the Cross, a procedure and an attitude comparable to a gnostic attitude. The Saint possesses, in the highest degree, the virtues considered necessary and indispensable for the realization of *jñāna.*

What are those virtues? The Upaniṣads distinguish four: the first is the distinction between the Real and the unreal, *viveka.* You see delineated here the way followed by the monk, finer than the edge of a razor. The Real, according to us, is the non-transitory aspect, the *Ātman,* which follows us like our shadow. The veiled intuition which we have of it becomes clear and distinct when we renounce truly what is transitory, that is to say, all that we have known until now.

For St. John of the Cross, reality is God alone. It is the *leitmotif* of the Carmelite convents. The example of this discrimination is furnished by Christ, in his life up to the Cross.

"We must conform ourselves to what he has done," St. John enjoins us. That distinction once established, one must realize it in life.

"It is no use to declare that thorns do not exist and then start to cry when one is pricked," said Sri Ramakrishna. It involves a life that goes beyond ordinary norms; the true monk of India does not stay three days in the same place. Like the integral imitation of Christ, this conduct realizes a perfect integration of man with the spiritual principle which he has discovered within him and which he considers to be the sole reality.

Discrimination, when it is real, rests on an illumination of the *buddhi,** this spiritual principle which is at the same time intelligence and will. It involves then quite naturally a transformation not only of thought but also of human conduct. That is why among the Great Beings who have "realized," we find such unity of thought and action.

> A soul is all the more united with God when she is more elevated in love, or when her will better conforms with God's will. A person who has reached complete conformity and likeness of will has attained total supernatural union and transformation in God," writes the Saint in *The Ascent of Mount Carmel.* (Bk II, Ch. 5)

St. John of the Cross offers us in his person the example of that perfect discrimination.

The second attribute necessary for the *jñānin* is the renunciation of all fruits of labour, here on this earth, and Beyond.

> Oh! If the souls devoted to spirituality knew what goods and spiritual favours they deprive themselves of, not wanting to detach themselves entirely from the trivialites of this world!

These words of the Saint are in complete agreement with the doctrine of yoga as set forth in the school of Ramanuja, for instance, where *bhakti* is tempered by a profound exercise of intelligence and by a method of purification of the lower part of man which St. John of the Cross speaks of as "night." "As transformation in God does not depend on the senses nor on human cleverness, the soul must strip itself *completely and voluntarily of all it might contain of affection for things on high and things here on earth.*" Such is the *vairāgya,* which St. John of the Cross calls "the stripping" and the "emptiness"* demanded for pure union with God.

One could say, however, that there remains a difference between the Saint's renunciation and that of pure *jñāna.* In the former, the soul frees itself from the desire for the things of this world but does not renounce, for all that, the joys of spiritual wedding and the beatitude of heaven.

St. John of the Cross says, in fact:

> Even when, little by little, she acquires *supernatural favours,* the soul must be careful to think of herself as stripped of them, to stay in the shadows like a blindman, supported by the obscure faith which is her light and her guide . . . , for faith is above all our knowledge, all our preferences, all our feelings and all our imaginings. (*AMC,* 5, 7)

This is indeed the way of "*neti*"* followed by the *jñānin.* Brahman is the negation of all that exists in this empirical world, and the affirmation of its existence can be realized only in negation and deprivation. "The road up the high mountain of perfection is steep, is narrow," says St. John of the Cross.

Up to this point there is full conformity between gnosis and mysticism. However, St. John of the Cross does not renounce the joys of heaven. In the union with God, the human is glorified. In the other life, the pleasure of enjoying the goods which the soul possesses is "perfect" (LF stanza 3, 79). It seems thus that the soul seeks here a new state of existence and, from the point of view of the Hindu *jñāna,* does not get out of the frame of māyā. To renounce that state of divine beatitude would be, in fact, for the Christian, the negation of all spirituality. That is nevertheless what the *jñānin* realizes when he establishes his life in an eternal present.

The third attribute includes a whole group of qualities:

> Tranquillity of mind: *śama*
> Self-mastery: *dama*
> Detachment: *uparati*
> Endurance: *titikṣā*
> Concentration of mind and faith: *samādhāna* and *śraddhā.*
> (*Viveka-Cūḍāmaṇi,* verses 22-25) (Śaṁkara)*

St. John of the Cross was tranquillity itself. He attained such a degree of calm that the suffering and misery endured in prison did not succeed in altering the purity of his spirit. That tranquillity was the result of the self-mastery he had acquired in the course of his asceticism and his detachment from all things.

"The repose of the mind applied to its end, once it has detached itself from the glitter of objects, by careful observation of how insufficient they are, is called *śama* or tranquillity."

"To turn the mind and the senses away from objects is called *dama* or self-control. When the mind ceases to respond to the attraction of objects, one calls that detachment or *uparati*."

"To endure all afflictions without trying to assuage them and to remain during that time free from anguish and complaint, that is called *titikṣā*, endurance." This endurance, which is found in St. John of the Cross, is not a natural quality; it comes from a continually renewed act of faith. It is confidence in God which creates in HIM a complete renewal. It is not a question of will.

"The acceptance by a firm judgement of the truth in which scriptures and the guru have instructed him, that is what faith is for the aspirant, *śraddhā*, by means of which ultimate reality is perceived."

Faith is not an obligation imposed on a Hindu in order to belong to a church. It is the desire for a superior life which creates a careful respect for the teachings of the sages. Faith is a spontaneous opening of thought towards the supernatural. In man, faith is a prefiguration of wisdom. It implies not only that attraction for whatever passes beyond the frontiers of intellect but also an effort, a perseverance, the only sufficient means to give the aspirant the feeling that he is pressing towards the more and more effective realization of his spiritual ideal. *Śraddhā* is distinguished from Catholic faith, then, by a slight nuance. It is above all an interior experience which is acquired by contact with the great spiritual masters. Faith lived in that manner gives it concentration by itself.

"Not a simply curious thought, but a constant concentration of the intellect on Brahman eternally pure, is what we call *samādhāna* or quietude in oneself."

All these qualities are explained at length by St. John of the Cross. Speaking of the amorous favours which God grants the soul, the Saint insists on the way in which the soul must be prepared to receive them. Knowledge of God must be received "passively" in the soul according to the supernatural mode of God and not at all according to the natural mode.

> It follows that in order to receive the knowledge of God, the soul must be absolutely independent of its natural behaviour, *free, tranquil, peaceful,* and *full of serenity,* following the examples of God like the air which, the more light and heat there are, the more pure it is, more exempt from vapours, more

> purified, more calm. (LF, stanza III, 34, italics added)

Previously, the soul was *seeking*, discoursing and meditating on particular subjects. Now, that is to say a short time before achieving total union, it no longer has anything to do; it must neither want nor search but keep itself in a state of calm and serenity so that its emptiness calls on the immense generosity of God to fill it, "that pacific and tranquil good."

We say thus that it is by the intervention of *sāttvik* tranquillity that wisdom fills the soul "in a manner secret and peaceful." "The pure heart is like limpid and tranquil water on which the rays of the sun are reflected. That is why only pure hearts see God," said Ramakrishna.

But this peace is realized only by detachment, *uparati*.

> Thus the soul must not be attached to anything, not to any exercise of discursive meditation, not to the taste of any spiritual or sensible experience, not to any mode of action whatsoever. The spirit must be so completely free and independent of any created thing that thought, discourse, or any kind of pleasure would be an obstacle; I will add that if the soul disturbs this profound silence she must be careful to watch her corporeal and spiritual parts in order to hear 'the profound and delicate word which God speaks in solitude.' (LF, stanza III 34)

The *puruṣa* can be reflected only in the *sāttvik* mode of *prakṛti*. One cannot find a more perfect concordance and a greater harmony between the Christian attitude and that of the Hindu *jñāna yogin*. They use identical images to describe the virtues which lead to the threshold of supreme knowledge.

Detachment (*uparati*) and self-control (*dama*) must accompany that tranquillity. It is in this sense that John interprets the prophet Habakkuk when he says: "I will stand on my watch and fix my foot upon my fortress, and I will contemplate what is said to me" (HB 2:1). John adds this like saying: "I will raise my thought above all activity and knowledge belonging to my senses and what they can attain to as well as all which they are able to keep" (LF, 36).

But this concentration of mind—*Samādhāna*—is difficult to keep.

> The most insignificant act is enough to disturb everything

> which the soul wishes to accomplish by herself, with the aid of its memory, understanding or will.

In this connection, a comparison with the discipline of *Rāja Yoga*, in the Hindu *sādhanā*, would be profitable. We shall return to this point.

That constant concentration on the eternally pure Brahman which our Scriptures advise is replaced in St. John of the Cross by an *obscure knowledge*. Since the understanding cannot know how God is, "it is thus necessary to approach Him as one defeated."

As a matter of fact, God surpasses all distinct knowledge. "He is incomprehensible and inaccessible to understanding." When understanding tries to act, it rather moves away from God. Thus it is necessary for understanding to *cease all operations*. (*Yogaḥ citi vṛtti nirodhaḥ*—stopping mental waves—is the Hindu definition of yoga.) In this way the mind is purified. But could one ask—and St. John anticipates the objection—what the mind is going to do? "Nothing," replies St. John. And it is then that it works most. It has a totally obscure knowledge, for "God, not being intelligible in this life, is a ray of shadow for the understanding" (LF III, 49). "What is night for all beings, is a time of vigil for the sage" (*BG*).

But—and this is an objection addressed likewise to a Hindu *jñāna*—one can love only what one knows, and what is a God without either form or character? In a word, how can one adore an impersonal God?

St. John of the Cross has a pertinent reply to that question. He begins by recognizing that the will can be inclined to love only by distinct knowledge. Love can be directed only towards what is perceived by the understanding.

But, he adds, "that is true especially when it is a matter of operations and acts that the soul performs naturally." It is no longer the same when it concerns supernatural matters.

When God acts and infuses Himself into the Soul, "it is not necessary that the soul have distinct knowledge nor that its intelligence be geared into action."[1]

---

[1] Brahman is really understood by whoever knows him as incomprehensible. He who thinks he understands does not know. Brahman is unknown to those who know." (*Kena Upaniṣad*, II,2) Or as Aristotle (quoted by St. John of the Cross) puts it: "Supernatural things are all the more obscure for our understanding when they are in themselves most clear and evident" (The Swami's note).

God sends love and knowledge at the same time; the mind has only to receive them in Peace. "It is a knowledge which is general and obscure," comparable to the light which diffuses without encountering an obstacle in an unlimited and serene space.

> The morning sun is ready to enter in your apartment as soon as you open the windows. This is how God acts in his vigil over Israel; *he does not sleep.* But he enters the soul which is completely detached from all creatures and fills it with its treasures. (LF)

Knowledge of Brahman is described in the same way in the Upaniṣads.

The light is always there. But is cannot penetrate us so long as we impose the forms of this empirical world between it and ourselves, forms which are like so many barriers to that realization of divine unity. "Grace blows ceaselessly," Ramakrishna used to say; "only set your sails."

God penetrates us, bursting all our barriers. If we don't understand Him, it is because He is comparable to a ray of sunlight which comes through the window. The cleaner the window is and free from dust and stain the less it is visible; on the other hand, the more motes and dust in the air, the more it seems perceptible to the eye.

> The explanation of this phenomenon, adds the Saint, is that we see light only by the reverberation that it produces around it; without that one would not see. For that reason, if a ray of sunlight enters by a window, and passes through the opposite window, it would cross the apartment without encountering any object and *there would not be any more light* than previously, and one would not see the ray. (*AMC*, Bk 2, Ch. 5, 6)

That is the way divine knowledge acts. Nothing can prevent its light from entering a purified mind if it is not stopped by anything: not being restrained by any particular object, natural or divine, it offers the mind the opportunity to explore the depths of the divine. "It is because he tastes and understands nothing in particular that he is well prepared to penetrate all" (*DN*, VIII, 5). It is in this way, adds St. John of the Cross, that the saying of St. Paul is mystically verified: We have nothing, and we possess all (2 Cor. 6:10). Such is the beatitude reserved for such poverty.

We find in Hindu thought an explanation of *jñāna* which bears an astonishing resemblance to the saying of St. Paul and St. John of the Cross. "It is true," said Sri Ramakrishna, "that the ordinary conditioned mind cannot realize God. But God can be realized by a pure mind (*śuddhamanas*) which is the same thing as pure reason, which is the same thing as a pure and unconditioned soul (*śuddhātman*). It cannot be attained by limited reason nor by a limited, relative, conditioned mind. But the mind can get rid of its sensorial nature, be purified by proper cultivation, and become free of all desires, attachments and tendencies of this world, to become only one, united with the unconditioned soul" (*Gospel*, p. 802). The *Ātman* is thus realized when no trace remains of the human being.

Ramakrishna compares the attainment of knowledge in man to a salt doll which plunged into the ocean: "As soon as it took one step into the ocean, it was lost and could no longer be seen. All the particles of salt it was made of dissolved in the sea. . . . The differentiated became one with the undifferentiated. This is what happens to one who has the happiness to realize the absolute God in the unsoundable depths of "*nirvikalpa samādhi.*" Śaṁkara compares supreme knowledge to the reflections of the sun on water contained in vases. Once the vases are broken, the sun's reflection can no longer be seen. Does that mean that it has ceased to exist? The absence of an object to shine on does not mean the absence of light.

St. John of the Cross thus finds the words of a pure *jñānin* in order to speak of divine knowledge. He believes, like the *jñānin*, that God is present in every soul and that He does not cease to be present in a substantial manner. This he calls natural union. In order to achieve the mystical union, what we call yoga, it suffices to transform that substantial union into a supernatural union or union by love.

Likewise, for the Vedāntic seeker of the Absolute, the *Ātman* is found is every soul: the *Ātman* constitutes the essence of the soul. The real human ego is *sat-cit-ānanda*, but man has to find his way back to that essential nature, and he can do it by the way of knowledge or the way of love.

"The true nature of man, of the *jīva*, is the eternal *Saccidānanda*.

But selfishness had raised so many barriers and limitations (*upādhis*) that he has forgotten his real nature," said Ramakrishna; and likewise St. John of the Cross: In order to unite oneself to that God who is already in one's inner self, "the soul needs only to rid itself of those oppositions and natural dissimilarities." It is then that God, who already has communicated with the soul through nature, will communicate supernaturally by grace. Those oppositions, those dissimilarities, we call *upādhis*, those envelopes of the soul which prevent unification with the Divine "I." *Sādhanā*, for St. John of the Cross, is thus presented in the same way as for the Hindu *jñānin*: it is a matter of lifting the envelopes and withdrawing from *mā yā*. "Since the soul is in God in an eminent manner as all creatures, God lifts a few of the numerous veils which she wears over her eyes so that she can see Him as He is" (*LF*, stanza 4, 7).

In St. John of the Cross, the soul can see God only through a veil, since the veils will not be *completely* lifted until after death. For the Hindu *jñānin*, as for the Christian saint, this divine vision changes one's view of the world. "The soul sees with a single glance what God is in Himself and what He is in His creatures; as one opening the gates of a palace sees at a glance the eminent person who lives there and what he is doing."

The soul sees God at work in his creatures. The soul sees how He works with them *by His virtue*: "It seems to the soul that she sees at the same time what He does, how He moves into the creatures, and how the creatures move in Him without interruption."

To the formless aspect seen earlier—that of light—in the thought of St. John of the Cross is added the formal aspect of the divine.

As Ramakrishna said, he who comes back from *samādhi* to the plane of sensorial consciousness sees all things afterwards as an expression of the divine. He keeps just enough of his individuality to preserve the spiritual vision.

He sees at that point *jīva* and *jagat* and himself as the One manifesting itself under multiple forms. That glorious vision, adds Ramakrishna, comes to the *vijñānin* who has realized *nirākāra* or *nirguṇa* Brahman in *nirvikalpa samādhi*.

"God, man and nature are the different faces of a single Reality. When you have deciphered one of them you can read them all."

We see that the realization of St. John of the Cross is very much like that of the Hindu *jñānin*. Like him, he recognizes the two aspects of the divine: *nirākāra*, the formless, and *sākāra*, with form. *Nirākāra* is not, however, necessarily *nirguṇa*, without attributes. God known in that state does not possess form but can possess all the virtues. If for St. John of the Cross He is "knowledge and love," for the Hindu *jñānin* He is *asti, bhāti, priya*: Existence, Light, and Love.

The fourth condition necessary for the aspirant to *jñāna* is an intense desire for liberation (*mumukṣatva*). St. John likewise points out that aspirants's desire: "My soul," said Job, "is languishing within me; it is all fiery without any hope" (Job 10:1). The cause, adds the Saint, is that the soul in a state of perfection, guided by the purifying night, is called to take possession of innumerable gifts and virtues. As a whole, the soul must see itself and feel remote, deprived, and stripped bare of all goods, like a stranger.

Sri Ramakrishna compared such suffering to that of a burglar shut up in a room where he senses the presence of a bar of gold in the next room. He has only to break down the door to take possession of all that wealth, and he is tormented by not having it.

St. John of the Cross is not only a candidate for that divine knowledge—he is a man who achieved the supreme height, the *yogārūḍha*, the heights from which one never falls.

St. John of the Cross is not a *jñānin* of the metaphysical kind like Maharṣhi; Ramaṇa Maharṣhi seeks *jīvanmukti*, liberation here on earth. That liberation does not appear as a passage from one state of existence to another, but rather as an inclusive union of all states, the realization of the One in all states.

What St. John of the Cross seeks, in accordance with his theological education, is a mode of existence, a liberation from this life, into the divine. We call *videhamukti*, a man who rises up towards a supreme state of existence after the disappearance of the body.

For the Maharṣhi, there is no future. "Being is; non-being is not." He will not emerge from this eternal present. It is the Being which acts under multiple appearances; death does not bring a greater revelation to the *mukta*.

For St. John of the Cross, even when the soul succeeds in the transformation of the spiritual marriage, the most elevated state one can attain in this life, the union is never "perfect nor absolute."

Complete transformation is accomplished only after death in glory (*SC*, XI, 10).

To sum up, we can say that St. John of the Cross is a *jñānin* in this sense: that taking as his base a radical discrimination (*nityānitya-vastu-viveka*), he rises to a formless knowledge (*nirākāra*) of the divinity. This knowledge is presented as a rupture of the intellect's normal framework, and an infusion of the divine principle in Serenity. That knowledge has for us the divine principle in Serenity. That knowledge has for us the three characteristics which make it supreme: *asti-bhāti-priya*: Existence, Knowledge, and Love.

Although these three terms hold a different significance for our two theologies, there is no doubt whatsoever that it is by them that we can best express the radiance of St. John of the Cross's mystical experience and the conquest of the Absolute which he realized.

4

Bhakti-Yoga and St. John of the Cross[1]

We have seen how we can to some extent consider the doctrine of St. John of the Cross as a yoga of knowledge, that is to say a union with God through opening the heart to receive the illumination of intelligence. Today we are going to study that doctrine from the point of view of love and show how the role love plays in Hindu thought finds parallels in the mysticism of St. John of the Cross. Love for us is the basic dimension of Being, when one considers its intangible and infinite nature. Being is love, just as it is "existence and light." It is *asti bhāti priya.* These determinatives are inseparable. In the secret of pure knowledge, Being appears as existence, light and love at the same time, love being also the supreme Bliss (*ānanda*).

Like God in Carmelite thought, the Lord is described in our language as "that essence of ecstatic love of which no one can speak" (*anirvacanīya prema svarūpa*). God is love, and love is the supreme means for reaching divinity. Whatever way one chooses, nothing is accomplished if one does not know charity, St. Paul says (1 Cor. 13:3). These words translate Hindu thought exactly. He

[1]This lecture was delivered at the Sorbonne on April the 9th, 1949.

will try in vain to be a puṇḍit who believes he has realized "Being as Being" and pure consciousness beyond temporality. If we do not know love, that supreme love which is the source and sap of our being, we will have realized nothing. In love we live and move and have our being. We are rooted in love. That is why love is the design made by the woven threads of our existence. No one can live a single instant without loving or without the hope of being loved. Only love can give us the feeling of a complete life, for only love allows us to live in unity.

Thus to love or be loved is nothing other than to recover our true being and to live in the very womb of reality. Love is, in fact, the unitive life and hence the perfect life. It is supreme Bliss. *Ama et fac quod vis* ("Love and do what you will".) (St. Augustine, VIIth Homily, *Homilies on I John.*) This claim is the basis of pure Christian mysticism, for whoever truly loves can never really go wrong. Also has it not been said that to love greatly is to pardon much? One who loves truly is always in the Truth. "Keep the knowledge of *advaita* in your pocket and do as you wish," says Ramakrishna. *Advaita* is complete knowledge, with no dualism between us and bliss. It is life in a love victorious over dualities.

Actually, love is a difficult conquest. It asks us to go beyond personality. We cannot love and stay the same as we were. In order to love we must transcend ourselves. Our life, in fact, insofar as it remains special, is cut off from the life which is truly *one.* Closed within the limits of our personal existence, we can no longer be irrigated by the main current of Being; we are, so to speak, diverted away from love. Before losing ourselves in the quicksand of egoism, the current is stopped. We find this stagnation of life in ourselves unbearable. We feel that we have lost love. But actually we can never lose it completely. It is recalled to us by an uneasy feeling of incompleteness, a suffering we experience when we discover we are only half living. The proof of love's existence is the dolorous trace which its absence leaves on our sensibility. Feeling it obscurely within ourselves, we long to possess it in its entirety. "You would not seek me if you had not already found me." Such is the word which comes to us in the intimacy of that eternal quest. But we do not know in its entirety what it is we possess.

The reason is that we do not know the real Self underlying our fragmented and scattered individuality. The *Ātman* flows out of itself through thousands of pores, revelling in the spectacle of multiplicity. It is lost from sight, mingled with that multiplicity. In this identification with different envelopes (*kośas*), the different personalities appear like masks hiding the face of the Supreme Reality. From that point on, all the effort of spiritual life consists of unmasking the face of Being which shines through the veils. Its beauty impregnates everything that passes. As creation bursts forth, the joy of its love does not cease to sing.

It is moreover what St. John of the Cross says in the 'Spiritual Canticle':

> Pouring out a thousand graces
> He passed through these groves in haste;
> By looking at them
> By his face alone
> He left them clothed in beauty. (V)

In searching for love outside ourselves, we seek it in its reflections, the multitude of names and forms which, like a bursting rocket, scatter and disperse. Excited by its presence in our inner self, we rush towards it and then are in despair at the futility of our chase in the "manifested world":

> Where have you hidden,
> O Beloved, and why have you left me sighing?
> Like the stag, you fled
> After wounding me.
> I went out calling for you, and you were gone. (I)

A day comes when this failure throws us into despair:

> Henceforth send no more messengers to me
> Who cannot bring the answer I desire. (VI)

The soul discovers that love is entirely present in each particle of the manifested world. For "indivisible, it appears as though divided into a multitude of separate beings." "That knowledge is *sāttvik* which distinguishes the same indestructible substance in the womb of separated beings." Thus speaks the blessed Lord in the '*Gītā*' (*BG* XVIII, 20). But in order to discover that, the soul must first be found in the inner self, in the silent and solitary chamber where the Beloved has led her:

> In the inner wine cellar
> Of my Beloved, I drank. . . . (XXVI)

It is then that she will see that in all she loved, it was He she was loving; for just as pure Consciousness is provisionally hidden by the images it projects in dreams, so the real rope is momentarily taken for a serpent in the illusion of a frightened man, and so Being has never been absent under the illusory, motley appearance of multiple, transitory forms:

> It is not, my dear, for the love of the husband that the husband is loved; it is for the love of the *Ātman*. It is not, my dear, for the love of the wife that the wife is loved, my dear, but it is for the love of the *Ātman*. (*Bṛhadāraṇyaka Upaniṣad* II, 4, 5)

Once the *Ātman* is realized, the soul understands that there had never been anything other than the *Ātman* everywhere, the sole being to be loved:

> My Beloved is like mountains,
> Like solitary wooded valleys,
> Like strange islands,
> Like rivers of thunderous water,
> Like murmuring zephyrs filled with love. (XIV)

The discovery of Being wholly present, although hidden in its effects, is difficult only because that discovery asks for a collaboration of the whole man. Not just an effort of the intelligence but a purification of the heart. The knowledge of love is a knowledge of the life at the centre of our being, and that "depersonalizing" knowledge is a knowledge that purifies. The heart works at it as much as the intelligence. The bliss of love is attained only in a "complete act" which leaves no room either for wandering thoughts of the past nor for the heart's aspirations for the future. All the powers of Being are collected and converge on a present intuition of infinity.

This immersion of the Supreme Being is a return to the source of the created. "I sought you in public places of the world, and I found you nowhere." He who wants love must dip into the fountainhead at its source and emerge from the manifested world:

> If, then, in the public square
> From this day hence I am not seen nor met with,
> You will say that I was lost
> That going my way laden with love,
> I thought myself lost, but I was found. (XXIX)

Knowledge of *ānanda* is attained only by transcending superficial joys, by a stripping away of the envelopes which constitute our different personalities:

> In solitude, she was living;
> In solitude, she made her nest;
> In solitude, her Beloved led her
> Self-wounded with love in solitude. (XXV)

The greatness of a created being, says our poet Rabindranath Tagore, consists in the fact that it is vitally linked to infinity. Man in his essence is not a slave but a lover. It is in love that his accomplishment and his liberty reside. Only love, in uniting him, with the Divine, gives him universal understanding. Without love, life loses meaning. Life without love is a restless suffering and a moral torture. "The soul which has not achieved the perfection of love has not achieved union," says St. John of the Cross in the *Dark Night*. "It hungers and thirsts for what it lacks—union." Unity alone is truth: "All is united in *ānanda*, truly. All beings are united in love. They live in love. At the end of evolution, they return to love." It is in this loving consciousness of God that the *ṛṣis* of old lived. It is from that consciousness that the Upaniṣads draw their inspiration.

Just as the musk deer discovers in dying that the perfume he was running after emanates from himself, so we discover that the source of *ānanda* is in us. But we can discover it only in dying. For the Beloved does not let himself be captured in the mirror of a particular personality. The bride must not love: she must become love: which is to say that in stripping away the different personalities which serve as masks, she must find a place in her centre, in pure being:

> Listen, O my God, to what I say.
> This present life, I do not want it.
> I am dying because I do not die. (*Stanzas of the soul that suffers with longing to see God.*)

Bhakti-Yoga is the science of opening the heart. It is by way of the heart that we attain the "mystical wisdom" which, according to St. John of the Cross, is itself a product of love (*Prologue to the Canticle*). So we see that love not only teaches us truths: it also makes us savour them.

The *Bhakta* is a person who seeks to realize unity through love. What draws him to the Lord is not power *per se*, but the power of loving and being loved. The *bhakta* seeks to perfect himself in love for the good of love itself.

Before arriving at that stage, he begins by loving in order to conform to the Scriptures and in order to put himself in harmony with a logical conception of the divinity he has constructed. The devotee is still "Green" (*gauṇi*); he needs to mature. The devotee considers it simply as a means to enable him to obtain bliss one day, in *svarga*, in heaven. That love is nourished by rites, ceremonies and sacraments, and warmed by the conversation of pious men. It grows also through prayer, silence, a healthy life, and meditation.

However, one gradually comes to like devotion. Little by little it becomes an end in itself. Concentration of the mind on an ideal object gathers together the real powers. The strength and the perfection which emerge from the object of contemplation are communicated little by little to the devotee who meditates on them. The ideal becomes a living, intuitive reality. Between the ideal and the devotee a kind of identification is produced by a slow ascension to the level of contemplation. During the first stage the aspirant must lead the fight against inferior instincts which threaten at each instant to upset the new order. Here love manifests its active virtue. Love only can suffice to deliver the individual from his harmful tendencies and implant a new direction in his nature.

This purification is aided by what St. John of the Cross calls discursive meditation, that is to say persistent reflection on a given theme related to the ideal. This mental rumination produces new habits which aid spiritual development. That is also the purpose of liturgy, sacrifices, alms and the repetition of the name of God:

body and soul must contract the habit of divine service. When these practices are carried out with vigilance, which is to say in full consciousness of their value, the whole nature of being becomes *sāttvik*; it is purified of what remains of animal tendencies and establishes itself on the plane of the greatest peace. St. John of the Cross warns us, however, against the damage that abuse of external practices can do to a soul when they are performed without discernment. In *Mount Carmel* he analyses very subtly the pitfalls into which aspirants may fall. Thus the soul can make use of devotion as a means of self-satisfaction. When the soul begins to devote itself to the Lord, in fact, "It experiences great consolation in religious exercise." The soul is like a young child completely surrendering itself into the arms of its mother: God makes the soul effortlessly find the sweetness of spiritual milk. He carries it on his breath, which distills for her tenderest love. From that moment on, the soul finds its delight in spending entire nights in prayer: "All its inclination is towards prayer, its joy is in fasting. . . ." These practices are certainly not useless: those who give themselves up to them assiduously profit thereby, but from the spiritual point of view: "One must know that the soul is conducting itself in a manner very weak, very imperfect, for it resorts to the pleasure they give and not to the love of God which alone should count." The soul is in quest of itself and brings to its practice a host of imperfections corresponding to the stage it has reached.

These aspirants, flattered by the happy state in which they find themselves, do not wish anyone to be good except themselves, and they take the liberty of condemning their neighbours. Such spiritual pride is a defect beginners sometimes fall into. Others discuss spiritual questions endlessly. They will go out "only surrounded by *Agnus Dei* and the relics of the saints." This attachment to forms is very far from spiritual poverty, and the saint condemns it as a kind of avarice, which is one of the cardinal sins.

There are others who feel sensuality stir in the very midst of their prayers; this body, insufficiently purified, participates in its way in the exaltation of the soul, and that participation produces disorderly passions.

Some, disoriented by the dryness which they suddenly encounter in the service of God, let themselves be overcome with anger. Unbearably disturbed, they attack God, indignant because they cannot make any progress. All these defects are summed up in a kind of spiritual greed which pushes one to want to "taste" God; more than purity of heart, they seek spiritual savour and believe they have experienced an emotion in their devotions.

Still others show envy and laziness. All such beginners must undergo the "Purification of the Night."

Speaking in the same line of thought, Ramakrishna pointed out the different nuances through which *Bhakti-Yoga* passes; the *bhakta* finds himself more or less impregnated with *sattva,** *rajas** or *tamas,** according to the spiritual temperament of the aspirant. "There are loves which manifest in the humility of *sattva*, others in the ostentation of *rajas*, and still others in the brutal force of *tamas*."

The *tāmasik* worshipper has a violent faith; he takes God by force, like a thief seizing what he covets. He cries out: "What! I shout his name and yet remain a sinner! But I am his son! I have a right to inherit his riches!" (*Gospel*, 146f). His faith is vehement.

The *rājasik* worshipper displays the distinctive signs of his religion: he carries a gold rosary; he is very scrupulous about external practices; he wears silk vestments at religious ceremonies and celebrates festivals and feast days with pomp and splendour.

The *sāttvik* worshipper carries out his devotions in secret; he meditates on his bed, behind his mosquito net, and consequently sleeps late in the morning, which his friends explain as insomnia; he will tolerate no luxury of dress or food in his house. He who attains *sāttvik* love is on the top rung of the ladder which leads to the divine; he will not have to wait long to attain consciousness of God.

> The faith of every man takes the form which gives him the substance of his being, O Bhārata. The faith in incarnate beings is threefold in kind like all things in nature and varies according to the quality dominant in each: *sattva, rajas* or *tamas*. (*BG*)

Thus the blessed Lord explains in the *Gītā*, and adds:

> *Tāmasik* is the ascetic practice in a dark spirit, imposing on himself suffering and effort. *Rājasik* is that which is carried out to obtain honour and consideration from me; it is unstable and ephemeral. But the sacrifice offered without desire for any personal gain, that is *sāttvik*.

This quality of *sattva*, or purity is enough for us to admit all forms of worship offered to the divinity; far from rejecting exterior manifestations, images or sacred objects (which would be the tendency of St. John of the Cross), we venerate them as salutary aids, a kind of divine language which is exchanged between the devotee and the divinity; very few men can achieve perfection without the help of images. The image habituates the mind to thoughts of God, introduces God into the very interior of matter. The image is valuable for the impetus it gives.

For us, God is above all a person, a being with divine attributes filled with purity. Beneficent radiations of his strength transform and lift up our personality. By adoring and worshipping his image, our every gesture, our every breath, becomes purified. Life loses its narrowness and its egoism, for the Lord incarnates himself in each act and lives in the heart of the devotee whom he has spiritualized. This life lived in the intimacy of an incarnate God is the essence of our religious devotion.

The great *jñāna-yogīs*, after having realized Brahman without attributes, return to this incarnated adoration of the divine. The "Image of clay is made of spirit." Just as "the toy, in the form of a fruit or an elephant, makes us think of the real fruit or the real elephant," so the images which we worship make us think of the God who is eternal and without form. "These images," adds Sri Ramakrishna, "are concrete forms of the essence which is eternal and without form."

Thanks to this mode of thought, in India great liberty reigns with regard to images in worship. This aim of *bhakti* is the transformation of our acts into offering and adoration. Infused contemplation—that is to say, the possession of God in continual prayer—can take place only if our entire personality has become *sāttvik*; that is why we are recommended to pray without ceasing. The repetition of the Divine Name purifies the deep levels of our person, and without our realizing it raises us up to a level of calm where we see things with the utmost clarity.

According to the degree to which we make ourselves more and more able to capture its light, the love we have for divinity intensifies: "When the worshipper takes one step towards the Lord, the Lord takes sixteen towards him."

The worshipper is like those courageous sailors who spread their sails and navigate, taking advantage of the wind. They arrive much more quickly than those who sleep on the ocean of life, forgetting that the wind of grace never ceases to blow. It is thus that *gauṇi-bhakti* is transformed little by little into *parā-bhakti* (pure devotion); the latter is the full flowering of religious feeling. Ramakrishna tells us how his devotion to God evolved:

> Each day, I would decorate the image of the goddess Kālī with flowers and sandal paste. For me it was not an inert image but Mother Herself, the repository of virtues and all blessings. I looked to her as my supreme guide in all this obscurity and confusion. Little by little the vision of the Divine Mother became my unique passion. Religious chants seemed to open the sluices of my heart and I wept like a child deprived of its mother: 'O Mother, where are you? Reveal yourself to me. Ramprasad saw you and obtained your grace. Am I rejected that you will not come to me? My only desire is to see you, Mother! (*GM*, 162)

The anguish of separation from the divine began. Ramakrishna would rub his face on the ground in pure agony.

"The more the desire for God augments," writes St. John of the Cross, "the more the soul feels itself carried towards God, burning with love for him." The soul does not understand, moreover, where this affection comes from; the soul sees its love grow to such a point that it begins to desire God with an anguish close to agony. "The more Rādhā approaches Śrī Kṛṣṇa, the more she feels the sweet perfume he exhales; the closer you approach God," adds Ramakrishna, "the more your heart is inundated with love and blessings for him" (*Gospel*, 277). But love, as we have seen, is the expression, on the level of sense, of the fundamental unity which is at the root of all beings; love aspires to union at the same time that it aspires to recover its original integrity. "The special virtue of love is to lead to the union, the junction, the equality, the resemblance with the loved object in order to perfect itself in the good of love itself," writes St. John of the Cross in *Dark Night*. "That is why love gives each of us new strength. Much more, as the saint accurately notes, it gives the soul, still miserable and plunged in purifying shadows, enough boldness and presumption to aspire to union with God."

Devotion to God must, sooner or later, result in a "hunger and thirst" for mystical union. This hunger and thirst are "Love's restlessness." "As the lioness or the mother bear seeks with anxious power the cubs that have been taken from her and which she will not find, so this wounded soul runs in search of its God." The image used by St. John of the Cross tells us that love is nothing other than the most complete possession of ourselves, repossessing what belongs to us. God, said Ramakrishna, is our own good:

> I tell you truly, God belongs to us. Pray to Him thinking that He is dearer to you than yourselves. He is more attached to his worshipper than the latter is to Divinity.

This union the soul finally desires with extraordinary force, with all the strength which emanates for the pure nature of recovered being, not yet conquered in the night which is the separation of the soul from created being.

> It is the voice of my beloved,
> Here he is, he comes:
> Leaping on the mountains,
> Bounding on the hills.
> My beloved is like a gazelle
> Or a young stag.
> See him, he is behind our wall.
> He looks through the window,
> He looks through the lattice,
> My beloved comes and says to me:
> "Arise, my love, my fair one, and come away!
> For now the winter has past,
> The rain is over and gone,
> Flowers appear on the earth.
> The time for singing has come.
> Arise, my love, my fair one, and come away!
> (*SS*, 2:8-13)

Such are the words which God softly speaks to the centre of the soul which has given itself to him. The soul then replies:

> My Beloved is mine and I am His.
> (*SS*, 2:16)

> On the mountains which separate us,
> On my bed at night,

> I sought Him whom my heart loves,
> I sought Him and I found Him nowhere:
> I will arise and roam through the town . . . .
> (*SS*, 3:1)
>
> The watchmen on their rounds at night met me:
> 'Have you seen Him whom my heart loves?'
> (*SS*, 3:3)
>
> They struck me, they wounded me,
> They took off my veil;
> I charge you, daughters of Jerusalem,
> If you find my beloved:
> What will you say to Him?
> Say that I am sick with love.
> (*SS*, 7:8)
>
> I am my beloved's and His desire is for me . . . .
> (*SS*, 7:10)
>
> For love is strong as death.
> Great waters cannot extinguish love
> And rivers cannot submerge it!
> (*SS*, 8:6-7)

The *Song of Songs* describes for us that impatient love, that love which must have the object of its wishes or die. "If the love which you have for God," Ramakrishna would say, "is as strong as the three passions combined, you are certain to reach God: the love which a sensual man experiences for the things of this world, the love which a miser feels for his treasure, the love which a pure and devoted wife experiences for her husband."

Just as "the rosy dawn announces the sunrise, so an ardent thirst for God in our hearts precedes the divine vision." The whole science of *Bhakti-Yoga* leads to the love for Him and the taste of His sweetness. "He is the sweet syrup, and the devotee is the bee which drinks its nectar." The relationship, moreover, is reciprocal. God runs towards his worshippers at the same time as they hasten towards him. "Just as the worshipper cannot live without God, so God cannot do without His worshippers. Then it is the worshipper who becomes the lotus and God becomes the bee. He becomes sweet in order to taste his own sweetness" (*Gospel*, 87).

Such is the explanation of the divine play of Rādhā and Kṛṣṇa. It is in this sense that we must understand that twelfth stanza in which St. John of the Cross has the Groom say:

> Come back, my dove,
> For the wounded deer
> Appears on the summit of the hill
> Drawn by the breeze of your refreshing flight. (*SC*, 12)

The Groom, adds the saint, is compared with the deer, for the deer always returns when he hears his companion groaning. Hearing the soul groan, he himself is wounded with love. This fact has been noted between people in love: the wound of one becomes a wound for the other. If the Bride is wounded by love, the Groom in turn is wounded by love for her. It seems that God desires to be set on fire by the fire for love which is released from His Beloved, for the soul's desires call forth His own desires. "It is by violent love," says Ramakrishna, "that the worshipper makes God come down to him. When the child abandons his games and weeps and calls his mother, she can no longer stray away from him" (*Gospel*, 241).

One cannot achieve *bhakti* so long as one does not have the feeling of already possessing Him. This feeling alone is enough to make sensual pleasures seem insipid: "If one day you attain the adoration of the lotus feet of the Lord, if you have once experienced the joy of singing His glory, then the long battle to subdue the senses is over. The senses submit of themselves" (*Gospel*, 241). That is why Ramakrishna thought that *Bhakti-Yoga* was the *dharma* which suits our iron age. True devotion, in fact, brings with it the renunciation, the discrimination, the love of all creatures and the service of the saints. True devotion transforms this existence into a veritable song of joy. "As soon as one acquires the love of God." sang Ramprasad, "the world becomes an abode of joy." Certainly joy and sorrow will remain inevitable companions of this terrestrial existence, fruits of our *karma*, but the glory of knowledge and devotion never abandon the true worshipper of God.

How does one achieve that perfect devotion? By establishing the most intimate relationship with God. When two people scarcely know one another, a certain formality reigns over their conversation. But, as Ramakrishna notes, as soon as they learn more about one another, ceremony vanishes and their relationship is less and less concerned with exterior matters. We must, at whatever cost, establish intimate relationship with God.

What can this relationship be? The Hindu mystic distinguishes five kinds which are designated by the term *bhāva*: *śānta* is produced when the human soul is attracted by Universal Consciousness. The ego is annihilated under the invasion of *saccidānanda*. It is a state of that immutable peace in which the ṛṣis* of old lived. It is the nuptial bed of the Canticle where the Groom rests with his Beloved. The soul possessing all virtues in full strength lives in sovereign peace, a peace full of love which has the feeling of Truth.

> Like the calm night
> When dawn begins to rise,
> Like silent music,
> Like harmonious solitude,
> Like the banquet which charms and replenishes love. (14/15)

The soul rests quietly in the light of the Divine, in the solitude of the spirit of love. In this state of ecstasy, the soul is no longer coloured by sensual affections or self-love; now nothing is superior or inferior. The soul is plunged into an abyss where incomparable harmonies are heard, surpassing all earthly concerts. The spirit of God fills the whole earth, and the soul is satisfied. The Beloved is satisfied. Her Beloved is all that for the soul.

Dāsya is the relationship established between the servants and the master who is served and loved. A mother sometimes has this attitude, and the Bride as well. St. John of the Cross does not insist on this relationship, which one finds often expressed in the Old Testament.

Sakhya is the *bhāva* which exists between friends. It is the kind of love which the little shepherds nourished for Śrī Kṛṣṇa when they played and chatted with him in the groves of Vṛndāvan.

Vātsalya-bhāva is the love of a mother who gives all her life to her children. The worshipper can adopt, *vis-a-vis* the Lord, this attitude of the nursing mother. The Lord appears to him then as a little child.

Madhura is agreeable love represented in our Hindu mythology by Rādhā, the passionate lover of Kṛṣṇa. That attitude is found throughout the work of St. John of the Cross. At first it is the languor of love which detaches the soul from all creatures and renders it insensible to all that is not God. "This weakness, this faintness, is the first degree which leads to God. Deprived of taste for things of this world, the soul finds neither support nor taste, nor consolation, nor repose in anything whatsoever." "Tears flowed continually from my eyes," says Ramakrishna, speaking of that first stage of *sādhanā.* "I would spend the day weeping, and when the evening bells announced the day's end, I would become still sadder and would begin to cry: 'Another day has gone by, Mother, and I have not seen you. Another day of this short life has passed in vain and I have not realized you' " (*GM,* 157). His plaintive cries drew crowds.

"When I sat for meditation a curtain of forgetfulness separated me from the external world. I was completely unconsious of those who gathered around me to attend the service. Often I remained seated for hours, repeating *mantras.* I even witnessed certain phenomena which according to some people are only phantasms of the imagination: for example, if I pronounced the mantra *raṅga* I would see a circle of fire spread around me, protecting me against all evil influence."

Eventually the soul no longer abstains from seeking God. Swooning with love it goes thorough the public square, seeking Him everywhere. In all that she says and does her sole concern is to find Him.

"I looked to Mother," says Ramakrishna, "as my sole guide in that obscurity and confusion. The vision of her divine form became my only passion." And the young priest would forget to finish the worship service, so deeply was he absorbed in his search; or he would run into the jungle, indifferent to all its dangers, and give himself up to meditation.

Having achieved this level, writes St. John of the Cross, the soul now considers unimportant the great things it did for the Beloved. The long time she devotes to Him seems short, "so ardent is this flame of love which she has already set afire." Moreover, the soul feels a profound desolation on seeing how little it can do for God; life seems wasted. The soul thinks herself the most miserable of creatures. "Oh, Mother, where are you? Show yourself to me! Ramprasad saw you and obtained your divine grace. Am I an outcast that you do not come to me? Pleasures, money, friends—I want none of them. I want simply to see you. Oh Mother!" (*GM,* 139). And the tears would flow in abundance from Ramakrishna's eyes, while his heart was torn because he could not realize Her.

This uncontrollable suffering is the fourth level of the soul's love, according to St. John of the Cross. It is a tireless suffering. The Bride of the *Canticle* said to the Groom: "Put me like a seal on your heart, like a seal on your arm; because love is stronger than death" (*SS* 8:6). The spirit acquires here so much strength, adds St. John of the Cross in his description, that it makes no more of a case for its body than a tree for one of its leaves. It is a very elevated level. The soul is so carried away with love that she moves constantly towards God.

An ordinary man cannot bear a fraction of this terrible fervour. Ramakrishna said that one would be reduced to ashes by only a quarter of that emotion. "For six years my eyes remained open. I could not sleep for one second. Looking into a mirror, I tried to force my eyes shut with my fingers in vain. Horrified, I cried out sobbing, 'Is this the result of my prayers, of abandoning everything for you?' But the next moment I would continue: 'Let it be as you will. Let this body fall to pieces, provided that you don't leave me, Mother. You are my only refuge' " (*GM*, 180).

At this period Ramakrishna rejected the sacred cord, sign of the Brahmin caste to which he belonged: for the soul must think of God, freed from all bonds, delivered from all attachments. "Don't you know," he said to Hriday, who was remonstrating with him, "that since our birth we have been bound by an eightfold bond of hate, shame, family, culture, fear, reputation, caste, and egoism? This sacred cord signifies that I am a Brahmin, hence a man superior to others. When I call to Mother I cannot entertain such ideas" (*GM*, 137).

An extraordinary impatience follows this stripping away. It is the fifth level on this ladder of love. The love which animates the Bride to seek the Beloved is so ardent, writes St. John of the Cross, that the smallest delay seems long, painful, unbearable. "My soul sighs and swoons in the sanctuary of the Lord," says the Psalmist. If the lover does not see whom she loves, she will die. She is famished, "a dog who prowls around the city of God."

"Are you true, Oh Mother, or is all this a creation of my brain, simple poetry without any reality? If you exist, why don't I see you? Is religion pure fantasy, a simple castle of cards? Life flies away in vain. Here one day passes after another, each lost forever; each one brings me nearer to death. Where is my Mother? Scriptures say there is only one thing to seek, and that thing is God. Without

Him life is an unbearable mockery. When God is realized life takes on sense, becomes a perpetual pleasure, a veritable garden of joy. What good is my life if day after day I drag a miserable existence without attaining the eternal source of immortality?" Such thoughts intensified Ramakrishna's desire and led him to redouble his efforts.

At this level the soul is nourished with love and satiated according to its hunger, as the saint notes; that is what gives the strength to mount higher. "Nothing except Her existed for me, I had to seek Her. I was going mad." The overflowing faith which sustained Ramakrishna was to make him succeed. It was no longer a matter of performing a ceremony seriously. "I would seat myself before Mother's image and stay like a stone, unconscious. I would act like one demented and weep like a child. People thought I was mentally deranged, but that did not bother me. All my energy was turned towards the realization of the goal I had chosen. Without food, hardly sleeping, my chest and face were always stained crimson by waves of emotion. A great fear was born within me—perhaps realizing Her was not part of my destiny. That thought wrung my heart like a wrung towel. Life was not worth the effort of living. I finally reached the point where I could no longer endure the separation." One day when he was in that state his eyes fell on the big sword which was kept hanging on the wall of the temple. "Determined to end my days, I jumped to my feet like a madman and seized it. At that precise moment, Mother suddenly revealed herself to me, and I fell senseless on the ground" (*GM*, 140).

"Preserved from all iniquity, I ran to you," says the Psalmist, and again, "I have gone the way of your commandments when you filled my heart." "Those who hope in God will take new strength; they will have wings like eagles." Such is the sixth level of love.

The seventh is an extension of the sixth. The soul, animated by a holy boldness, does not use deliberate judgement to wait, nor counsel to retire, for God's favours make it act with temerity. This is what the Apostle means by those words "Love believes all, hopes all, can do all" (1 Cor. 13:7). Such souls obtain from God whatever they ask. When this degree is obtained, the saint continues, the Bride of the *Canticle* is permitted to say, "Give me a kiss of your mouth." In this boldness and vehemence of love, attaining the eighth level, the soul is taken by the Beloved, who unites with it in the manner of the Bride of the *Canticle* who sang: "I have found Him who loves my soul and my heart. I hold Him and will not let Him leave."

"What happened after that," says Ramakrishna, "I am incapable of saying, but within me flowed an uninterrupted flood of constant joy, and I felt the presence of the Divine Mother" (*GM*, 141).

At this degree of union, the desire of the soul is satisfied but not in a constant way. For if the soul remains in that state, it will enjoy a kind of glory on earth. That is why as soon as it arrives it must withdraw. "From that moment on, I had nothing but the ardent desire to see Her again. For the divine vision was not continuous. It was only in meditation and with much effort that I succeeded in attaining it." For Ramakrishna's anxious heart, these failures could mean only one thing—that the first vision was not true. Could it indeed be that this thirst for God had not impregnated his whole heart? Such thought made him redouble his prayers. "I have given myself up to you. Do with me what you will."

The image of Kālī was regarded previously as a stone image, filled with supreme Consciousness, but now it was the Divine Mother who appeared to Him. The separation between them vanished. In this intimate communion Ramakrishna forgot all the formalities of the Scriptures. Love flowed from his heart in an uninterrupted flood. The divine Presence never ceased to be a reality.

It is this stage in the mystic scale that St. John of the Cross calls the degree of the perfected ones, those consumed by love for God. The Holy Spirit communicates to them "that love full of sweetness and delight, that love which is the cause of their union with God."

This degree Ramakrishna called a state of divine intoxication in which he realized the different *bhāvas* we spoke of befores the different possible relationships with God; it would take a whole book to describe his experiences.

These led him rapidly to the tenth level of the mystical ladder, where, according to St. John of the Cross, the soul is assimilated totally in God and enjoys his "clear vision" in an immediate way. When the soul has attained this degree there is nothing left except to leave the flesh, adds the saint. Purification on this earth is complete and "as love has carried out the purification of the soul, it does not have to go to purgatory through which other souls must pass ." "Blessed are the pure in heart for they shall see God."

"At this period in my *sādhana*," recounts Sri Ramakrishna, "I tried to think, according to the instructions of the *śāstras,* that sin was burned out of me, and that I was pure and perfect. I began to feel a burning sensation all over my body. One day when I was practicing in the *pañcavaṭī,* I saw a man with red eyes and black skin come out of the body and run over here and there like a drunk man. A little later, another man came out, dressed in ochre, carrying a trident. He attacked the first man and killed him. A few days after this vision, the burning sensation, which had been tormenting me for six months, left me" (*GM,* 148f).

Who can doubt that each of us holds hidden within him a personification of the evil which must be exterminated?

This total purification permits the clear divine vision. There exists, then, a perfect similitude between the soul and God. To express this idea, the saint takes up the words of St. John: "We know that we will be like Him" (3:2). This expression, adds the saint, does not mean that the soul will be as powerful as God—that is impossible; but it does mean that it will resemble God in every way. Thus one can call the soul God by participation.

This state of supreme devotion we call *mahābhāva*: we find it fully manifested in Sri Ramakrishna. Every devotee who came in contact with him saw in him the full manifestation of divine power. He lived in that state which St. John of the Cross calls no longer human but divine. Now he had to do only with the Absolute. The experience of Ramakrishna seems like an illustration of the description given by St. John of the Cross.

This comparative study permits us to affirm how much the levels of love expounded in mystical theology resemble the graded experiences of *Bhakti-Yoga.* The stages passed through seem the same, accomplished by the same sustained effort. As for the goal, ineffable to our intelligence, it is described in both cases as "assimilation" into God. According to the words of the mystical theologian, "love is like fire: it always rises towards the heights in order to attain the centre of its sphere." Bhakti-Yoga is thus a return to the source, an immersion in that Supreme Being which is *saccidānanda*: existence, knowledge, bliss.

Among the routes traced by *bhakti* in order to realize that supreme action, that of St. John of the Cross is the most difficult, and also the highest. The soul to whom God is represented under the colours of the Beloved strives to establish with him a love relationship ever more free and ever more charged with tenderness. The soul is not interested in knowledge or power; only one thing holds it and encourages it to be: it is to realize this love with more and more sweetness. The intense fervour of its longing is comparable to that which a lover full of charm creates in the heart of his beloved. It knows neither restraint nor barrier.

This love without bounds, truce, or rest, is magnificently described in our *Purāṇas* and especially in the episode of Śrī Kṛṣṇa and the shepherdesses. The *Bhāgavata Purāṇa* is the eternal melody of a soul enchanted by God. Like the Bride in the *Canticle*, Sri Ramakrishna began to experience a passionate love for the divine Śrī Kṛṣṇa. In a short time he had by this path equally realized a *sāttvik* devotion, that of Rādhā in Vṛndāvan, and he immersed himself into the Divine. It is thus that Sri Ramakrishna attained the culminating point of his spiritual ascension. There remained for him only the realization of *advaita*. The agony of the heart which lived through so many sleepless watches finally gave way to the glorious realization of the Lord. All his being was merged in that supreme bliss which comes from the realization of the Supreme Reality. Of Him one could say:

> The Bride has entered
> Into the garden of bliss so greatly yearned for
> And there she rests joyfully
> Her neck reclining
> On the gentle arm of her Beloved. (27/22)

> Those whose soul is great, O Pārtha, who live in the divine nature, they know me as the imperishable One, the origin of all existence, and knowing me as such, they turn towards me with a unique and undivided love. (*BG*, IX,13)

> The one who offers me with devotion a leaf, a flower, a fruit, a cup of water, that offering of love comes from the heart and is pleasing to me. (*BG*, IX, 26)

> Fill your spirit with me, be my lover and my worshipper, sacrificing to me, prostrating yourself before me: thus united in me you will come to me, making me your supreme goal. (*BG*, IX, 34)

Such is the definition of *Bhakti-Yoga* given by the blessed Lord in the *Gītā*. Besides love, what is the result of this unfailing yoga? The one who achieves it sees henceforth all things in *ānanda*. He sees things in relation to the Divine Principle at work in each of them. He sees all beings flow out projected by bliss. All beings are in *ānanda*: they are born from bliss, are sustained by bliss, and at the end of evolution, they return to bliss (*Taittirīya Upaniṣad*).

Ānanda, the supreme bliss, is Brahman. That bliss should not be confused with that which is experienced as an object of the senses. The later is only an infinitesimal part of the felicity of Brahman; it is that bliss manifesting itself through the intermediary of a terrestrial object. From the womb of this central perspective which includes all other perspectives, he sees beings advance in avenues, distancing themselves more or less from the centre of Reality. He sees them enclosed in the interior of their person like masks which hide their own identity from their eyes. One who lives in love possesses nothing but is at the heart of all things. "Henceforth he no longer guards the sheep; his sole occupation is to love." But in order to realize that love, a great devotion is asked of us. Love is a natural attribute of the Incarnations and the Sons of God. With them love gushes forth as from an inexhaustible spring where we all can come and quench our thirst. It is a torrent of milk and honey. The Incarnation, putting Himself in our place and relieving our *karma*, shows us how to see things as he sees them. An Incarnation infuses us with his light. Being at the centre of all perspectives, he has no particular point of view. The love he communicates to us lifts us to his level and we become capable of setting aside our ego in order to live in full generosity. Love tends to establish equality between one who loves and one who is loved. Giving and receiving love gradually brings us to participate in divine love. We learn to see naked reality.

> Whoever sees, O Arjuna, in all things equally, images of me whether joyful or sad, I consider him the supreme *yogin*. (*BG*, VI, 32)

Everyone should strive to reflect God; it is then that one can speak of divine communion, when the vessel of our person has become a simple receptacle for the strength and light which come from on high.

In the heart of the devotee this evolution is realized when the memory of temporal things is progressively replaced by that of the things of God (*smraṇa*). Action, whatever it might be, becomes contemplative. Then the devotee becomes an instrument in the hands of God. "Only become an instrument in my hands, O Arjuna," says the Lord in the *Gītā.* In such movement of his body, mental and physical, the devotee no longer sees anything but the Divine will at work in Creation. This state of consciousness, identified with that of cosmic force, is what we call *caitanya-samādhi,* the loss of self in total Consciousness. That state was realized by Girish Chandra Ghosh, the great lay disciple of Sri Ramakrishna, in the last days of his life. When some Swamis went to see him on his deathbed, and asked him what he had realized, he replied simply, "I am no longer I. In the simple act of raising my little finger, I see the Divine Will at work. The Divine Will directs all my thoughts."

In order to attain that state of *caitanya-samādhi,* the devotee passes through a stage of supreme abandonment of self. The least action of the self, whether it be discursive meditation or some other mode of spiritual practice, will be only a hindrance on the way, because in all these exercises a trace of self remains regardless of the degree of spiritual sublimation which has been attained. The infusion of God's grace is at work only when the devotee has attained complete passivity, through *ātmasamarpaṇa,* to use the term of Sri Aurobindo. This is a state of complete tranquillity, which is not the passivity of inertia but a divine passivity, the expression of an incandescent activity of the Divine at the interior of the self, when one no longer presents the least obstruction to its manifestation. It is the "action in inaction" of which Śrī Kṛṣṇa speaks in the *Gītā* (IV,18). Then only God descends into the soul of man, and man receives the supreme benediction of infused contemplation (as St. John of the Cross calls it).

In our mythology the story of Śiva abruptly leaving his wife, Pārvatī and going out of the room and returning after a short instant, is an illustration of the phenomenon of grace. Pārvatī was astonished. Śiva explained to her, "A devotee who was engaged in battle appealed to me for help. But when I descended, I found him defending himself. Thus he doesn't need me." If we give to the Lord the power of attorney for us (to use the language which Ramakrishna used for Girish), we should have confidence in the wisdom of his will and in the expression of his compassion. At that stage, *bhakti* becomes *Bhakti-Yoga;* God is united to man by drawing his soul into the Divine Consciousness.

5

The Yoga of Saint John of the Cross and the Theological Roots of Faith[1]

Applying the term yoga to Christian mystics risks misunderstanding. It calls to mind the Indian tradition of spiritual life. Is it proper to speak of yoga in the theological treatises of St. John of the Cross without falling into the confusion which any mixture of tradition inevitably involves? But if we use the term yoga without reference to any Hindu theological idea, if we restrict the term to its etymological meaning—union of man with God, the supreme principle—then it is altogether legitimate to speak of yoga in connection with the life and achievements of any mystic in any part of the world. The cultural background of the mystical experiences of saints varies according to the country of origin. Faith and dogmas have multiple expressions. Nevertheless it cannot be denied that among all the transformations of human life which

[1]This chapter was first published by the Vedanta Center of Gretz, France, in 1949 under the title, "Le Yoga de Saint Jean de la Croix." A somewhat abridged version of this chapter appeared in *Vedanta for Modern Man*, pp. 300-351, under the title "A Hindu View of Christianity." The translator is not named. This is a revised version of that English translation which restores omissions.

result from spiritual experiences, there are common points, even though the theological roots differ from case to case.

I want to make clear from the start that my aim is not to shake the convictions Christians have in their dogmas or their faith in a single revelation. In this study of St. John of the Cross, I am offering certain reflections arising from the confrontation of Christian theology with Hindu thought and culture, but in doing so I have always been clear that my task is not to reconcile the irreconcilable—though this does not prevent me from being aware at the same time that there is a possibility of finding affinities with Hindu mysticism in St. John of the Cross. The holiness of all saints is translated into love in the sphere of social relations. In all parts of the world men and women in the course of that realization of love experience psychological changes that have similarities we cannot ignore. Whatever the diversity of spiritual nourishment absorbed, their assimilation transforms its nature into love; thus there can be no dissimilarities if one perceives that love inserted into the texture of human relationships.

If we wish to understand the yoga of St. John of the Cross, we will find that it is impossible to set aside the edifice of his faith, and that leads us to an attempt to understand certain doctrines in the way they are received according to Christian revelation. The Hindu attitude towards all theology is one of respect. St. John of the Cross has given commentaries on Christian theological ideas which are among the most penetrating ever written. They are a marvel of thought, precision, psychological acuity, and spiritual beauty in their exposition of Christian theology tightly bound to the Christian code of living. It is only with the particular focus of Christian theology that we can follow the saint in his exposition of doctrine. But since this is a comparative study, we will not limit ourselves to following his own unique scriptural way. We will at times change glasses and observe him with our Hindu spectacles. These alternating points of view will enable us to understand better than a unilateral presentation of doctrine.

The root of all spiritual transformation is faith. The Christian's faith is in the Biblical revelation, the Hindu's is in the *Vedas.** Ideas of God, soul, and salvation differ, and to try to establish a forced identity would be fruitless. Revelation is sacred knowledge revealed from on High to minds incapable of penetrating the region of the supernatural. To judge revelation according to intellectual criteria is an act directly contrary to faith. The act of revelation is divine and speaks of matters beyond comprehension by the human mind. Śaṁkara says that given matters impossible to verify (for instance, the nature of our existence before birth and after death) Scripture is the only valid authority. If the Hindu accepts the possibility of revelations other than his own, he must find a means of reconciling his own faith in his own bible with other revelations whose truths contradict his belief. The approach the Hindu takes in that situation is to adopt provisionally the viewpoint of the other, to see as he sees, excluding momentarily his personal commitment to his own code of doctrines. This discipline, which consists of making the viewpoints of others his own, makes the Hindu capable of realizing a vast synthesis. That is not a sterile syncretism nor a cheap eclecticism, merely borrowing from different scriptures elements which complement one another. However, a civilization and a culture which are not habituated to this spirit of synthesis will not be able to appreciate either its value or its importance.

The synthesis that we speak of is the synthesis of all *dharmas*, of all ways of righteousness. But this term becomes an empty verbalism unless one refers it directly to the visions and realizations of the *ṛṣis*, the ancient seers of truth. Here is demanded of us faith in the great ones. Until we develop their vision ourselves, all that we see and know are only partial aspects of the truth. To have a global view with depth and profundity, one has to gain a new focus of adjusting the different perspectives. As in a stereoscopic view where two images appertaining to the two eyes are brought to a focal point that gives depth—a third dimension—so in the vision of the *ṛṣis* there is an integration of multiple perspectives; one who has realized Brahman becomes Brahman, and according to the *Gītā*, Brahman, ultimate reality, has an infinite number of phases. If the word "Totality" (*sarva*) is used, it must be understood that it does not signify a totalization on a numerical basis; in fact, reality surpasses the whole notion of number. It is a matter of a synthetic viewpoint from which is excluded all possibility of suppressing any aspect: that which the ignorant see as a part is seen by the sage as the whole. Different religions furnish different scales of observation and diverse perspectives, but the *tattva*, the truth, which is the centre of the vision of the Whole is extra-religious and is situated beyond all opinions. The expression of a realization of *tattva* surpasses a religious truth; it is a metaphysical truth. Whoever has realized that truth no longer sees any opposition between different theologies with the faiths which are founded on them and the truth harmonizing all the creeds based on the vision of totality. To stand in the shadow of one religious perspective only, excluding all others, would not give (according to *Vedānta*) that vision of *tattva* which is extra-religious. But to insist on the possibility of an extra-religious truth to those who have committed themselves to a religious truth does violence to their faith. The mere fact of admitting the idea of such a truth will constitute blasphemy in their eyes. That is why when we study a faith we must see the total vision, from the summit of which all religions appear as different paths to the same goal. In Christian faith, the intrusion of any perspective other than that strictly authorized by revelation would be an error which could only lead to heresy and confusion. Hence it is necessary, in studying St. John of the Cross, to remain in the axis of his own perspective. That is the only way by which we can gain access to the theology he adheres to. One of the greatest obstacles to the mutual understanding of Hindu and Christian concerns the content of the word "truth." When a Christian affirms that he possesses the Truth, he understands that term in its religious sense. If a Hindu uses that same word "Truth" in a discussion, he gives it an extra-religious value.

To St. John of the Cross, Jesus Christ is the only Saviour. Any union with God is impossible if this position is not accepted. As an article of faith, the Christian accepts the theology of the Old Testament, its view of the creation of the world, the picture it paints of sin, and its promise of a saviour whose sacrifice on the cross is to bring a unique answer to the problem of salvation. Accepting this major premise, we can understand St. John following a line of faith that is not the Hindu's, by proclaiming Jesus as the only son of God.

The prophets of the Old Testament communed and conversed with God. Through this dialogue between man and God certain truths were revealed. St. John speaks of this in his *Ascent of Mount Carmel*: "In olden times it was necessary to ask God things relating to faith, and they were revealed according to those supplications. With Jesus Christ, who is *Word* in its completed form, God has given us everything. He has nothing more to give us." "With the coming of Christ, God has become dumb, as it were, and has no more to say, since that which He spoke afore time in part to the prophets, He has now spoken altogether in *Him*, giving us *All* which is His *Son*." "That which God spake of old in the prophets to our fathers in sundry ways and divers manners. He has now, at least, in these days, spoken to us once and for all in the *Son*." "In this Son of God are hidden all the treasures of wisdom and knowledge of God." "He is all my vision and all my revelations."

The Hindu mind is accustomed to venerate many incarnations. Such a notion has no place in Christian theology. As if anticipating the position of those who believe in different incarnations, St. John writes, making, as it were, God speak: "But now, any one who would inquire of me after that manner and desire to speak to him or reveal aught to him would be in a sense asking me for Christ again; and therefore he would be committing a great offence against my beloved Son, for not only would he be lacking in faith, but he would be obliging Him again, first of all, to become incarnate and pass through life and death."

In the Christian view, the coming of Christ was for a definite purpose: to redeem man from sin. Humanity suffers from the original sin; human nature was polluted at a historic moment when the commandment of God was not obeyed by Adam and Eve. This sin has vitiated the blood of humanity: and no human agency can save it. There is the promise of the scriptures that God, incarnated as man, by his sacrifice on the cross alone can save humanity. Jesus Christ as the Son of God fulfilled this promise, and the way for establishing a new alliance was shown. The efficacy of the sacrifice made once for all time is the foundation of the faith for successive generations of mankind seeking to be liberated from sin. Wishing again for another incarnation is to doubt the validity of the sacrifice already made by Jesus. Jesus came to fulfil the promise of the scriptures. Every detail of his life runs on a pre-established plan, and he himself refers to the prophecy of the Old Testament as he enters into each new phase of his life. The cross is the way of salvation. To doubt the sacrifice that Jesus made is to wish another incarnation to go through all the suffering he underwent already. If he comes for a second time he has to pass through and repeat all the trials of his life once more. When the position of the Old Testament regarding sin and remission of sin through the blood of the Son of God is not respected, the foundation of Christian theology is doubted. That means lack of faith.

When a Hindu argues with a Christian about the possibility of many incarnations, he is probably unaware of the importance to the Christian of original sin. To insist that Christians should forsake that theological view of the fall of man is to show lack of respect for their beliefs. We must remember here that St. John, as a true Christian, reflects in his faith the whole position of the Old Testament. The notion of time in Judaic theology is static. Time was created and time must have a stop. It will end. Within this stasis the processes of history are dynamic. There is only one chance for man to fulfil his destiny. Man is born in sin, and he who gives him redemption from sin is the son of God, Jesus Christ.

I am thankful to the great Russian theologian, the late Professor Nicolas Berdyaev,* who explained this to me and enabled me to understand how the notion of time as conceived in Judaic theology is the key to the differences in the Christian and Hindu outlook. Time in Hindu philosophy is not static but dynamic.

By considering the Hindu attitude towards time, the Christian may be able to understand why the Hindu admits multiple incarnations. The Christian should hold in abeyance the Judaic position and try to see the problem within the background of Hindu philosophy and theology. Time is *māyā. Māyā* is not illusion. It is the kinetic aspect of reality. Śrī Kṛṣṇa says in the *Gītā,* "I am time." There is neither creation of time nor end of time, as reality never ceases to exist. Reality is existence. As time is one with reality, there is manifestation of time and non-manifestation of time. Time is *śakti* or power. It is cosmic energy having multiple forms of expression.

In *māyā,* with which it is identified, time functions in infinite fields of consciousness. On the human plane, when with death consciousness incarnated in a body ceases to function, human personality does not terminate its history on earth. It takes on innumerable embodied existences, in reincarnated forms, until all the *karmas* are worked out. As there is this upward movement of consciousness expressing itself through varied forms from that of a worm to that of the highly developed human being, there is in nature, in *māyā,* a downward movement of the divine taking human form without the shackles of *karma,* having power to liberate beings enchained by *karma.* This descent of God on earth is the advent of an incarnation. As time, with which the Lord is identified, is dynamic, having multiple expressions, so there is no prohibition of the Divine to reveal Himself in different periods of history. The purpose of the divine incarnation is not, as in Christian theology, to wipe away an original sin contracted on a historic occasion. The Hindu notion of sin is different. The word "sin" appears in the *Gītā* and in other Hindu scriptures many places. But there is nowhere in Hindu theology any reference to the effect that sin entered into man as an external force on a certain day when man disobeyed God. The notion that God comes in human form to take away sin is common to both traditions. In Hinduism sin is a deviation from the path of righteousness on the plane of conduct and morality. Disobedience is a moral error. But error is an obtuse interpretation of truth. There is no static quantity which is called "error." In empirical life all is relative, and truth is received according to a hierarchy of different points for viewing it. Each experience of empirical truth is an experience of the Real (Brahman) in its totality. Śaṁkara says that our experience of the universe is a constant perception of Brahman. Brahman is never experienced in fragments because it is indivisible. But in empirical experience, when the experience of the real on the one plane is contradicted by that on another plane, from the point of view of the superior plane, that of the inferior plane appears as an error.

There are thus several degrees of truth on the empirical plane. When the *sādhaka*, the aspirant in spiritual life, does not perceive any contradiction in his experiences, then the Supreme Truth (*pārmārthika sattā*) becomes a term interchangeable with the real. Truth is then an intuition: it is the consciousness of *turīya*, "The eternal *IS*." The shadows of error extend or are reabsorbed in function of that retracted light which is empirical truth, whose shadow is relative ignorance.

For the Christian, redemption from sin is the way which leads to liberation; for the Hindu, freedom from ignorance is the objective of the spiritual quest. If the word "sin" is continually repeated in Christian theology, so in the Hindu language the term ignorance is repeatedly pointed out as the barrier separating man from his immortal heritage, which is the knowledge of *Ātman*. In Christian theology there is only one way for man to be redeemed from sin. In Hindu thought there are numerous ways leading to the destruction of ignorance. The route offered by the coming of a particular incarnation is only one of those ways. There are systems of thought, such as *advaita vedānta*, where the aspirant to spirituality has no need to accept the theology of *saguṇa* Brahman, in which the theme of the *avatār* plays the most important role as saviour of humans.

It is not so much disobedience to spiritual authority, but rather ignorance of it, which is the cause of deviation from the path of righteousness (*dharma*). The promise of the Hindu scriptures is that the Divine will take human form to reestablish the scale to spiritual values. The Divine accomplishes this mission, not by centering on one single event in his life — like the passion or the resurrection in the case of Jesus — but by infusing into a decadent world a mass of spiritual power that radiates to all who are blessed to receive it; in individual lives the level of consciousness is heightened in various degrees.

The incarnation is an ideal man; he sets the model for others to follow. This mission of the incarnation commences from the very beginning of his early career, unlike the life of Christ where his power to liberate man from sin comes only after he had fulfilled the promise of the scriptures, when the cross has become the effective way of salvation. From Bethlehem to Calvary, in the Christian view, was only preparation. The disciples and followers of Jesus were prepared by him from the moment he began his mission for the supreme event of his life, his sacrifice on the cross. The Son of God became the saviour of humanity in the moment of his crucifixion. It is faith in this that saves. St. Paul says: "If any angel from heaven preach any other gospel unto you than that which we men preached unto you let him be cursed and excommunicated" (Gal. 1:8). After quoting these lines, St. John of the Cross adds further: "Wherefore since it is true that we must ever be guided by that which Christ taught us, and that all things else are as nothing, and are not to be believed unless they are in conformity with it" (*AMC*, II, 22, 8).

Thus what the Hindu considers to be the *intransigence of Christian faith* is for the Christian the *necessity to obey his faith and to put it into practice.* If a Christian who belongs to the Church starts believing in multiple incarnations, he takes Christ out of his historical frame and builds on him a new theology which is the result of a mixture of traditions.

But the Hindu, who incorporates Jesus Christ within his notion of many incarnations, will not do any violence to his tradition.

He will not be mixing up traditions. It is well-known that Sri Ramakrishna had an experience of Christ, but the Hindu does not say that he had a Christian experience. To have a Christian experience, according to the tradition of the Church, one must accept as an article of faith the dogmas and the credo of the Church. Expiation of sin, by participating in the passion of Christ, results in union with God; man broke his promise and the possibility of a new alliance was established by Jesus Christ. No one can commune with God except through Christ, who alone has the power to reintroduce man to God. St. John the Evangelist is formal on that point. The notion of that God is the Biblical idea of Him. Sri Ramakrishna had the Vedic experience of divinity, totally different from the Judaic one. He did not seek union with the Judaic view of God: *he had already experienced* God as Hindu mystics have from time immemorial.

According to St. John of the Cross the highest state that man can aspire to and realize on earth is the state of union, known in mystic language as spiritual marriage. This is the state St. Paul attained when he said, "I live, yet not I, but Christ liveth in me" (*Gal.* 2:20). In the words of St. John of the Cross: "According to this likeness of transformation, we can say that St. Paul's life and the life Christ were one through union of love which in heaven will be perfectly accomplished in the divine life of all those who shall merit being in God." This spiritual marriage may come to pass in this life as in the case of St. Paul, but, in the words of St. John, "*Not, however, in a complete and perfect way.* The spiritual marriage is the highest estate that can be attained in this life, for everything can be called an outline of love by comparison with the perfect image of transformation in glory" (*SC,* 12, 8). In the *Ascent of Mt. Carmel* this idea is more clearly indicated: "We shall see, we have not, we cannot have permanent union in the faculties in this life. We can only have a transitory union" (*AMC,* BK 2, Ch. 6, 1). Complete union is possible only in heaven, in the spiritual, glorified body.

This corresponds to one of the several ways of liberation of the Hindu, the notion of *videhamukti*—liberation that comes after the death of the body. But the theory of "jīvan-mukti," the liberation which can be attained only during our life on this earth, is quite different. So long as the body lives, a human being, according to Christian theology, is not exempt from the possibility of sinning.

That is why no great soul, no matter how saintly, can be canonized while alive. According to the Hindu way, perfect liberation from all impurities that come from the inner carnal impulses can be gained even while here on earth. Perfect union with God, which in the view of the Christian is possible only in heaven, is possible for the Hindu while on earth. For the Hindu—since he does not believe in original sin—is not compelled to regard the material body as being irrevocably polluted and, even if purified by rituals and ceremonies, always running the risk of becoming at any moment prey to Satan.

Ramakrishna experienced Christ a long time after he had realized God. In Christianity, the believer takes refuge in Jesus Christ in order to attain union with God. Christian scriptures insist on the point that no one can reach God save through Jesus Christ, but I do not believe that it is said anywhere that it is impossible for the unbaptized to have contact with Christ. When Paul had his experience of Christ in a vision, he had not yet been baptized: the experience of Christ came first. Once having become a Christian, St. Paul incorporated his acceptance of Jesus into the framework of Judaic theology, the only theology he was familiar with. In that basic theology he found the elements of his own civilization and culture which permitted him to translate his acceptance of Jesus in the form in which all his teachings proclaimed the message of Christ. Ramakrishna had an experience of Christ in the rich background of his civilization and culture, where there is room for multiple incarnations. Ramakrishna did not adhere to the Christian theory that there can be only one incarnation. For him, there was no theological obligation to take account of the salvation announced in Christian scriptures. He had in fact experienced Divine Consciousness before he experienced Christ. As I have already said, for the Hindu the incarnation is of God Himself and not only the son of God. In Hindu scriptures, nowhere is an incarnation designated as the Son of God, and one will not find any affirmation like that of Jesus: "I and my father are one" (John 10:30).

The theory of multiple incarnations is not only a theory but is also a fact intimately related to another fact: the soul is offered possibilities to work out her *karma* in the course of multiple lives. The Incarnation takes on the *karma* of the disciples, but there is no dogma by virtue of which the Incarnation must suffer in order to bring about redemption which is offered to suffering souls. And yet this notion of vicarious expiation is not altogether foreign to Hindu thought. In the case of Ramakrishna, we know that he suffered because he accepted the transference of his disciples' sins. He undertook the expiation of their imperfections. One day Swami Vivekananda asked this question: how can the Master suffer, since he is an incarnation of the Divine Mother? Hearing the question, Ramakrishna prayed to the Divine Mother and then had the following vision: he saw opposite him another Ramakrishna, bathed in celestial light and full of good health and vigour. Before him stood a long cortege of disciples. He touched them one by one as they came and prostrated themselves before him. One after another he saw them delivered from their sins, having attained perfect illumination. At the same time the transference of the *karma* of his disciples appeared on his body in a subtle form of ulcers. These eruptions gathered into his throat and provoked the visible illness from which he suffered. In this way he knew that the illness was not due to *this* own *karma*, but to the acceptance of the *karma* of his disciples. Sri Narayana Bhatta of Malabar, a great saint and philosopher of the sixteenth century, transferred to himself the leprosy from which his guru suffered. He wrote on that occasion his famous *Nārāyaṇīyam*, which is a summary of the *Śrīmadbhāgavatam*, and at the moment when he finished his work, he was cured. One can find in the Hindu tradition many other examples of vicarious expiation. We see here a universal fact, recognized in all parts of the world; hence it is not Christianity which introduced the idea of vicarious expiation, and Jesus Christ expressed in his life one of the laws of spiritual transformation of the disciples, that of the expiation of their transgressions in the person of the guru. Kṛṣṇa died as the result of an arrow wound, but that death was not the central event of his life. Our theory of salvation is not based on the way the incarnation dies. In order to understand the Hindu idea of incarnation, we must always bear in mind the fundamental principles of the Hindu philosophical perspective; and it is totally different from the Christian point of view. For the Christian, man is the centre of the created universe—an anthropocentric point of view. The Hindu idea, on the other hand, is cosmocentric. The incarnation resolves the problem of personal attitude or impersonal attitude with regard to life. The incarnation lives in *bhāva-mukha*, the borderland between the relative and the absolute. It is the reality simultaneously *nitya* (eternal) and *līlā* (relative). In the *Gītā*, Kṛṣṇa gives to Arjuna instructions for meditating on his cosmic aspect. In the *Śrīmadbhāgavat* there is a detailed description of the methods in the form of Kṛṣṇa with this cosmic symbolism, where different parts of the body are identified with the different quarters of the cosmos. The incarnation is the Vedāntic infinite, one with *Īśvara,** *Hiraṇyagarbha,** and *virāṭ,** God as the primordial cause of the universe, God as cosmic consciousness, and God as the cosmic concrete universe.

The impersonal is not a negation of the personal. It is seeing the Divine Person in the personal, the vision described in the *Gītā* by the words *Vāsudeva sarvamiti.* It is to know that everything is the Lord. It is to succeed in attaining what is known in mystical experience under the name of *mahāhāva.* This experience can appear as a vision of the Lord present in all things under the aspect of the Chosen Ideal, as the gopīs saw Kṛṣṇa; or seeing in Him the whole universe, as did Yashoda when she looked into the mouth of the infant Kṛṣṇa, or yet again, as Arjuna contemplated him in the cosmic form of *virāṭ-rūpa* described in the eleventh chapter of the *Gītā.*

After having surmounted the limits of the personal point of view determined by what we call the *purūṣa tantra* (individual approach), reality is presented under the aspect of *vastu tantra* (reality as it is) which is no more polluted by *saṁkalpa* and *vikalpa* (imagination). This reality as felt and experienced by mystics can be with or without form. The experience of the impersonal is not limited to the realization of the formless. The impersonal as experienced by Arjuna and Yashoda had cosmic form. The same Reality is also experienced by mystics as formless. The impersonal as formless is realized in the experience of union with cosmic consciousness (*hiraṇyagarbha yoga*). According to Christian theology, the mystics' experience of the formless is considered as the expression of the transcendent aspect of Reality. In the dualistic traditions of India parallels to the Christian ideas of transcendence and immanence can be found, but, according to *advaita vedānta* and the spiritual experience associated with it, transcendence does not pertain to reality. The latter can never be modified and nothing can be predicated of it; to define it would be to limit it. If we say that Reality is *sat* (existence), *cit* (knowledge) and *ānanda* (bliss);

or else *asti* (being), *bhāti* (light) and *priya* (love), the Vedāntic implication of these terms is that reality is not *asat* (non-existence), that it is not *acit* (absence of light), and that it is not *nirānanda* (deprivation of bliss). Śaṁkara has repeated many times that the purpose of the Upaniṣads is to teach us that all conceptualizations regarding Brahman lead us to error. Thus to say that the supreme Reality is transcendent is, in a sense, to limit it. Reality remains self-revealed when ignorance has gone. If the idea of transcendence can be applied and used, its only application is on the level of vision coloured by the ignorance of the aspirant to truth. It is this vision that changes, and reality remains ever as it *is*.

According to the Hindu outlook we have to note two perspectives. One is the vision of the universe by the Lord; this is expressed in a concise form in the tenth chapter of the *Gītā*. The other is the vision of the devotee. Among the various ways of experiencing the reality by the spiritual aspirant we can note three principle modes. These are expressed in the words of Hanumān: "When I have the consciousness of my body, O Lord, I am your servant. When I feel I am a creature with a thinking mind, I am a part of you. When I realize that I am *Ātman*, there is no difference between you and me."

A Hindu who reads the Bible will want to find these three approaches in the Christian Scriptures, and he will try to discover in the words of Jesus formulations of familiar ideas. But satisfaction is not proof of truth, and when we approach Christian Scriptures, we must penetrate to the very core of that tradition in order to find out whether Hindu ideas can retain their validity there. The initial error committed by Hindus, in trying to force identification, is to attribute to Jesus the vision of aspirants. Jesus Christ is one with God. He does not belong in the category of disciples. His words are divine authority; his vision is that of God. He is not a simple *yogi* —he is more; or, if that term *yogī* can be applied to him at all, it is in the sense we give it when we say that Kṛṣṇa is a yogī. The word "yogī," as it is generally used, is applied to one who is a *sādhaka* (an aspirant practicing spiritual exercises) or else a *siddha* (one who has attained the perfection of yoga). "I and my Father are one" (John 10:30); or "I am the true vine and my Father is the husbandman," (John 15:1)—to want to read into these sayings a sense approaching *advaita* or *viśiṣṭāvaita*, establishing identities thereby, does violence to Christian theology. The cosmic approach and the notion of relativity underlying the theory of *māyā* are not characteristics of Christian theology. For a Christian, the tenth chapter of the *Gītā*, which describes the vision of the universe as seen by the Lord, will be considered pantheism, which is one of the greatest heresies condemned by the Church throughout the ages.

Although in India we accept many incarnations we must consider nevertheless the personality of all incarnations as *one unique* person. The *Gītā* makes this point very clear in the fourth chapter. Śrī Kṛṣṇa says that he remembers all his past incarnations. In our ordinary human life that which gives unity to our character, building around a solid psychic centre, is memory. If there is a loss of memory, or disturbed effects of it, then there is no connecting link between the past and the present. On the contrary, if the thread of memory is not broken, there is a continuity of personality. Kṛṣṇa had this continuity of memory identifying himself with past incarnations. Ramakrishna had the same continuity when he identified himself with Rāma and Kṛṣṇa. Through the unifying force of memory the identity of the incarnation as *one unique person* is established. He is not the only son of God to the Hindu; he is the only person, the person of God, that takes human form. The etymological sense of personality derives from the word "persona" or mask. The Lord puts on different masks, as Kṛṣṇa, Rāma, Chaitanya, Ramakrishna, and others. He is conscious of the identity of the different personalities within his cosmic individuality. The word "individuality" (coming from the Latin word that expresses negation plus the word meaning to divide) has the significance of indivisibility. He is, as the *Gītā* says, indivisible, but appears as if he is divided.

Whatever view the spiritual aspirant takes, be it anthropocentric or cosmocentric, it is the faith he has in his theology that is important. So long as faith works and transforms our character, and particularly when that faith is traditional, depending on revelation, we have no right to question its validity. Let us take an illustration. Taking either view, the heliocentric or the geocentric—the sun-centered or the earth-centered—an eclipse can be predicted with exact precision. An identical result can be obtained through the use of modes of calculation diametrically opposed to each other in their conception of the universe. In the same manner, whatever may be the difference in theology, when faith works, the result is the same— a transformation of character!

Scriptures are the words of God. Theology aims to make their meaning more intelligible to us, not to amputate them nor to suit them to human convenience. Each scripture has an integral internal unity; each is a harmonious whole. If this is true with regard to Christian theology, it is equally true with regard to Hindu theology. Śaṁkara, Ramanuja, and Madhva strained their best to make the Hindu scripture systems of thought where there can be no discrepancies. They did not permit a certain section of the scriptures to be considered as true and others as having less validity. As revelations, the assigning of degrees of value to the scriptures is not warranted by orthodoxy. Swami Vivekananda accepted this position, and did not consider that the harmony of scriptures created a problem in making values; but he considered scriptures as accounts of spiritual experiences and theological viewpoints.

Each position is *Integral.* To raise the question of *values* means to establish *relations* between two or more positions according to their degree of importance. Each view takes the problem out of its setting vital to the individual. Each plane of reference has to be accounted for separately within the particular angle of the individual's mode of outlook. The contents of one food may be richer; but so long as I am not eating it, its existence is of no value to me, and the fact of accepting another's food—though richer in value—will be inappropriate.

So it is with regard to spiritual discipline and the theology inspiring that discipline. Sri Ramakrishna's spiritual experiences confirm that view. When he followed the Islamic way, he could not for the time being accept modes of spiritual practice that conformed to the Hindu outlook. But the question of superiority or inferiority did not arise in his consciousness. Spiritual disciplines are for the transformation of character, to reach levels of consciousness different from those available in our mundane existence.

Theologies are not for hair-splitting intellectual manipulation. They form instead the real foundation of faith. Dedication to spiritual life comes out of love for the ideal. When love is transformed into faith, that faith becomes dynamic. We start doing a thing out of love for doing it. When there is no love, work becomes tasteless. The more we do a thing with our heart in it, the more confidence we get in what we do; for an act done with love is creative, and in the dynamism of creative work, our faith in what we do increases.

In spiritual life the end we seek to gain is love of God, which is infinite. Acts of adoration through love leave in us more and more hunger for the infinite, which can never be expressed through words that are finite. This produces a wringing of the heart that pants for the infinite, in the way Sri Ramakrishna suffered when he cried out, "O Mother, another day is gone and thou hast not revealed thyself to thy child." The spiritual aspirant, not having yet tasted the integral experience, who still continues his acts of adoration, gains the *certitude of that state* through faith born of love for the ideal. Faith thus becomes the guiding star in his life and love for the Chosen Ideal—but not love as a sentimental outburst of a momentary feeling and satisfaction in that feeling, which are grave dangers in the spiritual path, according to St. John of the Cross—is expressed through acts that the scriptures ask us to conform to. Thus Śrī Kṛṣṇa says in the last verse of the sixteenth chapter of the *Gītā*: "Therefore, let the scriptures be your authority in determining what ought to be done." Again, in the third verse of the seventeenth chapter, the Lord says, "Man consists of his faith; he verily is what his faith is."

This faith is divine; it is blind because it does not operate through the mind. The mind, according to St. John of the Cross, works through *discursive meditation*; then when faith becomes ardent, man is blessed with *infused contemplation*. The spirit of the Lord infuses itself into the human soul, and the soul has nothing more to do. She has only to remain, in the words of Brother Lawrence, like a mass of marble allowing the chisel of the Lord to fashion her. We find the same idea expressed brilliantly in a Vaishnavite work from South India: *Śrīvacanabhūṣaṇam*.

This dynamism of faith breathes into life and plays beautiful melodies. Only one totally dedicated could abandon his person like a lute for the Lord to play upon. All real mystics composed celestial music, the melodies that wrought a magical effect, first on themselves and then on those who heard them. The melody is the eternal refrain of *love*. But the essential thing is the music and not the science of music. In Hindu musical science there are major melodies (*rāgas*) and minor ones. But the terms "major" and "minor" do not imply value judgements so long as the music is good. In the *rāga* called *haṁsadhvani*, there are only a few notes in the ascending and descending scales. But this *rāga* can be developed with as much depth and subtlety as any other rāga, such as the *śaṁkarabharaṇa*, where one finds seven notes in ascending and descending scales. The music produced by Christian saints like John of the Cross and Teresa of Avila is as sweet as that of any Hindu saint; but it does not have the notes which we are accustomed to hear in a major *rāga*. For example, we do not find that cosmic viewpoint nor the theory of reincarnation, nor the idea that humans, and with them all creation, are born in *ānanda* rather than in sin. In the music of Christian theology creeds and dogmas are notes essential for the faith. If we listen to occidental music, we must keep far from our minds the scales of the Hindu *rāgas*. If we consider a particular theology, we must not allow the shadow of another theology to be projected onto it. Composite images may be helpful in discovering a particular norm; but to want to proceed thus in the science of spirituality will lead to confusion and produce discordant notes.

It is by the word of God—which is revelation—that the seed of faith is transmitted. If love becomes dynamic through the action of faith, it follows that a live faith, in the sense in which the word is used in the letter of James, cannot fail to produce love for God. Love and faith in fact become interchangeable terms. They have identity in their inner significance, and the distinction in the use of terms is one without a difference. The light that illuminates man is the light from God. Man, bound in sin according to Christian thought, can be liberated from it only through the grace of God. The question of free will and predestination, of individual exertion and the gratuitous gift of grace, which are matters of such awful import tc Christians, particularly Calvinists, do not disturb the Hindu. The fact of humans having successive lives on earth through the fact of the balancing power of *karma*, in the construction of an equilibrium between the negative and positive forces operating in life, reveals itself in the soul through the growth of a higher intelligence. This higher intelligence has its seat in God; and when human ignorance goes, man will discover that all dualistic notions are illusions. With the destruction of the structure of this illusion, the particular dualism between free will and predestination, between human effort and grace, will also disappear.

The absence in the Christian outlook of the notion of *karma* and successive lives gives it an accelerated tempo. Human destiny has to find its fulfilment in this very life. The Christian has no time to lose, and what has to be done has to be done here and now, the only passage on earth. The notion of many lives makes the Hindu take his time more easily, breeding often lack of earnestness; he is not in a hurry as he has infinite time before him to work out his salvation!

One of the articles of the Christian faith is the second coming of Christ. That event can happen only when the whole world is evangelized in the name of Jesus Christ. The conversion of the pagans is a preparation for the second coming of Christ, the parousia. Let us examine how the modern Hindu reacts to this so that he too can preserve his faith. If the missionary zeal is born of faith, the Hindu reaction towards it is an awakening in the Hindu masses of a consciousness of the essentials of spiritual glory; in short, it would make Hinduism dynamic. The word "aggressive" Hinduism has to be replaced by the term "dynamic" Hinduism, for the word "aggression" smells of violence and enmity to the opposing school of thought. As the Hindu respects all faiths, the Christian is allowed all freedom in India to exercise his mission. But the Hindu would be *lacking in faith* if he allowed the *dharma* of the Hindu soul to be violated by outside forces, permitting it to die under the menace of another faith.

A powerful movement is slowly coming into existence to try to reintegrate into Hinduism those who, due to lack of vigilance on the part of those considered to be guardians of the *dharma*, have strayed away from the Hindu fold. To apply the word "reconversion," however, is an anomaly, for the ignorant masses have never been really converted to anything else. A solely external conversion to Islam or to Christianity is no conversion. Psychologically it is as impossible for a Hindu to believe that Adam and Eve are his ancestors as it is impossible for a Pondicherry schoolboy, who learns by heart from a textbook published for French children, that "the Gauls (our ancestors) had blue eyes"[1] to believe that his Hindu forbears had blue eyes! Manu, Prajāpati, and others are—according to his traditions—his ancestors. Real Christian theology can become a part of the Hindu's faith only

[1]From 1671 to 1954 Pondicherry was French colony.

if the subconscious mind accepts the first lessons in the catechism on the fall of man and original sin. Psychologically this is an impossibility.

In the experience of Christ of Sri Ramakrishna and through the Christian ardour of Mahatma Gandhi, the common man in India is alive at this critical point in history to the necessity of readapting the course of history in the same way India did long ago in assimilating the Buddhists back into the Hindu fold. This is done not through a fiat from some reformer, but as a result of an awakening from within. It is not a mechanical adaptation; it is an organic growth.

In the different chapels and sanctuaries where Hindu gods and goddesses are worshipped and in the temples, images of Jesus Christ and of the Virgin Mary will receive the homage of India's millions. If the word "pagan" is used for those who have no faith in the Christian dogmas to indicate his adhesion to his revelations and mythologies, then the Hindu is proud to reclothe that much abused word with an Indian significance and to call himself pagan, attributing to that word its original etymological significance (a peasant or villager). That will in some measure make retribution for the insults that have come down to him for so many centuries by allowing that word to be used against him in a disparaging sense. While the missionaries attempt to *Christianize* him[1] the Hindu has begun the process of *paganizing* Christ. He is adapting Christ within the background of his own cultural traditions, offering him worship in ritualistic forms that are familiar to him in the adoration of Kālī and Kṛṣṇa. Full freedom is given to the Christian to exercise his apostolate. For in the rich soil of the synthetic spirit of the Hindu, no violence is done by venerating Christ in the way he is accustomed to honour his gods and goddesses. This is the exercise of the Hindu faith. To recognize in Christ, as in all other divinities, a cosmic expression of *Īśvara, Hiraṇyagarbha* and *Virāṭ* (God as first cause, as cosmic consciousness, and as concrete universe)—such is the supreme achievement of the Hinduization of Jesus Christ. If this is not warranted by historical facts, nothing

[1]Since the Second Vatican Council, the attitude of Catholics towards non-Christian religions has changed radically from what it was when this lecture was given. Missionary work is no longer proselytizing but dialogue. A superb example of this dialogue is *The Marriage of East and West* by Bede Griffiths (Springfield, Illinois: Templegate, 1982).

is affected in the Hindu mind. He does not search historical evidences for spiritual facts that are not of this world.

The process of fulfilment in time, and an absolute value given to history—essential to the Christian because of the Judaic notion of the static quality of time—are not articles of faith in India. When Ramakrishna was told of the doubts of the modern educated mind as to the historicity of Kṛṣṇa, he replied that the fact that Lord Kṛṣṇa expressed himself in the lives of the mystics and devotees is incontrovertible evidence of his existence! The existence of a birth certificate for a spiritual hero does not confer on him a greater credibility than the Purāṇas have created; the Purāṇas make him live in our midst, here and now. Spiritual truths are higher than historical facts. Kālī and Gaṇeśa, Śiva and Hayagrīva, are not historical personages. No more are they symbols, as certain apologists or Hindu snobs try to explain to sophisticated Westerners. In order to understand these realities, one must acquire a new language of the soul. If someone suffers from Daltonism, he cannot recognize the colours the way normal people see them. We will not enter into vain discussions regarding the foundations of our faith. Proselytising and converting are activities altogether foreign to the spirit of Hinduism. To limit a spiritual event by keeping it within an historical framework does not satisfy the Hindu mind. Spiritual reality grows according to defined spiritual laws and comes to life in the experience of mystics; thereby our faith in these realities finds support. If, in the eyes of historians, there never was a Kṛṣṇa, born in the north of India, then travelling to the South, that in no way prevents his worshippers not only from having visions of Kṛṣṇa but also from finding actual evidence of his objective presence in south India. And it is important not to confuse these things with hallucinations or illusions. It is by a myth of this sort that a spiritual reality lives; no one can prevent it from doing so. No reforming zeal of modern propagandists can bring about any transformation when it is a question of a modern movement from the heart of the nation which takes by assault, as it were, the new forces, with the aim of adopting them to that vital zone of national existence which is the soul of the race.

In the European languages, two lives of Ramakrishna have attracted the attention of the reading public. One is by Romain Rolland,* who gives a careful historical version of the life of the Master. The other is by Dhan Gopal Mukerji,* called the *Face of*

Silence, where very few facts tally with history. Whenever I have met devotees of Ramakrishna in Europe I find it is the latter book they prefer, for Ramakrishna through this legendary version is more alive than through the research reporting of Romain Rolland. Yet we cannot accuse Dhan Gopal of having falsified the account of Ramakrishna. He made a Purāṇic version of the life, and a legend breathes a breath of life which the dialectics of a Śaṁkara or Ramanuja can never achieve. Dhan Gopal is an artist and the world owes more to the literary artists than to the bare biographers; Balzac when he fell ill wanted to be treated, not by a flesh-and-blood physician, but by the doctor he had created in his novels!

Spiritual personalites like Rāma and Kṛṣṇa get out of the framework of history; they really treat the soul that is sick and regenerate it into spiritual glory. They remain as the very salt of the earth. Mahatma Gandhi prayed to Rāma and through repeating the name of Rāma he got the power to awaken the masses of India. So, we believe that in India the power of Ramakrishna will operate a renaissance by giving the Hindu soul that alliance with its cultural past, which is nothing but faith in the mission of *sanātanadharma* (eternal law).

As I have said, the basis of love in spiritual life is faith. The *expression* of love is all important—not theories of love. This has been eloquently brought out in the second chapter of the epistle of St. James:

> If you fulfil the royal law according to the Scriptures, 'You shall love your neighbour as yourself', then you do well.
>
> But if you show favour to certain persons, you commit a sin, and the law itself condemns you as transgressors. For whoever observes the whole law, *but fails to keep one point of it is guilty of the whole*. In fact, he who said *You shall not commit adultery*, also said, *You shall not kill*. [italics added]. Thus if you kill, although you do not commit adultery, you are a transgressor of the law. Speak and act as those who are to be judged under the law of liberty. For judgement is without mercy for those who show no mercy; mercy triumphs over judgement. Of what use is it, my brothers, for a man to say he has faith, if he has not works? Will that faith be able to save him? If a brother or a sister is naked and lacks daily food and one of you tells them, 'Go in peace and be filled,'

> without giving them what their bodies need, what good is your blessing? It is the same thing with faith: faith without works is dead. But one could even say, 'You have faith and I have works. Show me your faith without works and I will show my faith by works. You believe in a sole God and you do well; the demons believe also . . . and they tremble. But be convinced, O vain man, that there is no virtue in faith without works.' (James 2:8-21)

Our works are the reflection of our faith; faith is supernatural. Adhesion to the Christian or Islamic credo is faith. Brahman cannot be known through the mind and its faculties. No spiritual life is thinkable without faith in the supernatural.

Dr. Suzuki* has shown in his essays on Zen that in Mahāyāna Buddhism, where there is not the least notion of a spirtuality tinged with deistic ideas, there is still a basic need for faith. It may surprise us that in the realization of the "void," (*śūnyatā* or Buddhatā, the state of Buddhahood, the state of *dharmakāya praveśa*, that is to say entrance into the body of *dharma*) one can attach much importance to faith. Words become surplus baggage in depicting a state that cannot be expressed in words. It can be attained only by an inner vision, the figurative opening of a third eye. To quote Dr. Suzuki: "Metaphysically speaking we can say that this constant appeal to the spirit of investigation is based on *faith* solidly established in the functioning of and the activity of the Buddhatā itself that conducts us to find out where the *one* sojourns."

Here is a Koan, one of those cryptic, incomprehensible formulas which the Zen master gives his students as subject for meditation:

> If all proceeds from the ONE, where then does the ONE reside? A Zen master says, 'Only where there is infinite faith will the spiritual effort bear fruit. Faith and the spirit of investigation which push the aspirant to accomplish his sādhanā are not contradictory things. Having faith in the ultimate termination of the sādhanā prepares the spirit so that all other superficial activities of the mind are suspended. The depths of consciousness are awakened and a power greater than the empirical ego illuminates total Reality. (Suzuki)

This faith in the promise of enlightenment is given in a paradoxically exaggerated form by the Zen master Lin-tsi:

> O you disciples of Truth, if your want to obtain an orthodox comprehension of *truth*, do not allow yourselves to be induced into error. Internally and externally if you meet with obstacles, mow them down. If you meet with the Buddha, kill him; if you meet with the Patriarch, kill him; if you come across an Arhat, kill him; do the same with your parents and ancestors without any hesitation, for that is the unique way for liberation.

The necessity to kill every dualistic conception, particularly the one that represents the chosen ideal, has been described by Ramakrishna in narrating his own experiences in achieving the *advaita* illumination. "As soon as the form of the Divine Mother presented herself before me, I employed the sword of discrimination to cut her to pieces."

If the reign of faith is fundamental in spiritual practices where there is no place for dualistic conceptions, how much more should we respect the importance given to faith in dualistic religions. If in the *advaita* approach one must have such a faith as to cut to pieces his chosen ideal — a procedure abhorrent in the eyes of *bhakta* — and if it is only on the basis of such a faith that all the tabernacles of thought and form can be negated to arrive at the ultimate affirmation, as Hindus we need not hesitate to give primacy to any form of faith, however dualistic, illogical, or irrational the content of the faith may appear to be. Negation means, equally the negation of negation, which is affirmation. Every faith is the language that God speaks in different countries and different epochs. It is lack of understanding of that language that creates want of comprehension.

Some years back I met a person in Geneva who was mocking Catholic ritual. Unable to suppress my indignation at this irreverence and knowing that no argument would be effective, I just stopped him and began to speak to him in my own language, Malayalam. Then I asked him in his language what effect my words had produced on him. He said that he had a mind to laugh. "Why?" I asked him. Because, he said, he could not understand me.

To understand we must know the language of the other person. We must be able to understand the foundations of faith of another who does not belong to our religion, and then only can we arrive at a vast synthesis, which is the harmony of faiths taught by Sri Ramakrishna. Sri Ramakrishna did not trouble himself to understand the various theological differences in faith. He exemplified the truth of faith by his various explorations into the spiritual realities of religion by making religion a matter of realization.

Faith in the supernatural, which is the integral and essential element in all the orthodox religions of the world, demands of us renunciation of our ego and our will. This renunciation of the will is the ideal of becoming *poor*. One is poor only if he is the idea by which one becomes really *poor*. As Meister Eckhart puts it:

> As long as you have the will to accomplish God's will, as long as you have a particular desire, even a desire which makes you soar towards the Eternal, you are not really poor. Only one who wishes *nothing* is poor.

Such is the sublime peak to which the yoga of faith leads us. The yoga of Faith is truly the *pūrṇa yoga*, integral yoga, in which all the other yogas (*jñāna*, *bhakti*, *karma* and *rāja*) are contained.

In the yoga of faith are contained all the other yogas. St. John of the Cross set such a supreme value on the realization of that poverty of which Meister Eckhart speaks. The word "*nada*" in Spanish means "nothing." How to arrive at this nudity of the senses and the mind is what St. John expounds in his theory of the Dark Night of the Soul. Understanding, will, and memory are kept in abeyance by rigorous ascetic discipline. From discursive meditation the soul is led to the region of infused contemplation. The soul realizes her union with God through faith, hope, and charity.

6

The Rāja-Yoga of St. John of the Cross[1]

1. Parallels

Rāja-Yoga is the royal road which leads to union with the divine. Use of the term "yoga" is legitimate when it is a matter of a school of religious thought, since it designates the union of the soul with God. Conceptions of God vary according to doctrine, but "yoga" includes all methods of approach, and each of them can rightly claim the use of the term. Moreover, one can even practice yoga in schools of spirituality which have no notion of God and do not formulate precise postulates concerning ultimate Reality. That is the case, for instance, with Buddhist schools. There yoga is assimilated into a psychological or parapsychological approach to Reality. That Reality is expressed, whether in positive terms for the *vedāntin* by the affirmation *All is Brahman*, or whether in negative terms by the Buddhists when they declare that from the beginning nothing exists.

---

[1]This chapter was originally published in the Fall of 1953 as an article in a special issue of the magazine "Cahiers du Sud". The article was titled "Le Rajayoga de Saint Jean de la Croix."

Yoga does not take sides and propagates no particular school of thought; it maintains an impartial attitude towards all its partisans; religious minds as well as those whose attitude is extra-religious make use of yoga as a means of approaching Reality, and each school remains entirely free to formulate, according to its faith, its own conception of Reality. We must, futhermore, envisage that method from a purely psychological viewpoint and not allow any theological or doctrinal consideration to blind us in relation to the human mind when in the course of its spiritual quest it determines to explore its capacities. The greatest possibility for a human being is certainly the power to impose silence on one's thought by the annihilation of the *vṛttis* (*citta-vṛtti-nirodha*): "yoga consists in preventing the mental content (*citta*) from taking various forms (*vṛttis*)" (second *sūtra* of Patañjali). Or, to use the words of St. John of the Cross:

> The soul, before attaining the state of perfection, must ordinarily pass first two main kinds of nights which spiritual writers call the way of purgation or purification, which here we call "nights" because, in both cases, the soul walks, so to speak, in night and darkness. (*AMC*, Bk I, Ch. I, 1)

In his prologue St. John of the Cross says: "Our Lord wishes to plunge souls into the dark so that He may lead them from there to the divine union" (*AMC*, Prolog, 3). A little further on he writes: "It is thus clear that in order to succeed in uniting oneself to God by grace and love while here below, the soul must be in darkness relative to all that the eye sees, the ear hears, imagination represents, and the heart perceives."

Concerning the realization of the Dark Night of the soul, St. John of the Cross writes: "We are going to prove how faith is a night for the mind. We are going to speak of obstacles which faith encounters and of *the active role which faith itself must undertake.*" Hence we read: "Such is the spiritual night which we have called active because the soul *depends on herself* to pierce it" (*AMC*, Bk II, Ch. 2, 3).

We italicize these words in order to indicate clearly that, according to the yoga of St. John of the Cross, the disciple must engage in a certain amount of activity. These words of the saint serve as a response to certain critics of yoga who claim that yoga does not adapt to Christian mentality and is directly opposed to

Christian theology, for (according to these critics) the disciple is incapable of taking any action leading towards spiritual advancement; since the soul is contaminated from birth by original sin, no human effort is efficacious for redemption and only divine action can save. The theologians who raise these objections insist that the disciple is incapable of taking an active part in his spiritual progress; they insist on the necessity of complete submission to the will of the Lord. St. John of the Cross would reply that such an opinion clearly denotes a misunderstanding of the proper attitude for a disciple. On the other hand, the criticisms of those theologians would be perfectly applicable to the second stage of spiritual life, when the active role of the soul is terminated; that is to say, as soon as the soul has gone beyond the purgative way. She now enters a passive state, according to the saint. The passive way includes what the soul does not do by itself nor by its own diligence, but what God does in the soul which then becomes, as it were, passive. More than once the critics I referred to have stated that yoga is nothing but a kind of culinary recipe which their Christian theology could never accept. We advise them in all seriousness to read the doctrine of the Dark Night and the description of the active role the soul takes before the Lord introduces Himself in the second stage, the passive stage. This second stage is that of infused contemplation; here the activity of the soul no longer has a part, and it is there that our theologians could legitimately try to oppose yoga. But in the last stage of spiritual life, yoga accords the highest importance to complete renunciation of the human will; the soul then remains entirely passive. That degree is, according to the Vaishnavite Schools, a union with the divine called *savikalpa-samādhi* (a state of union where duality subsists). According to the teaching of a great spiritual master of South India, one of the great Ālvārs,* the soul then becomes like a block of marble in the hands of a sculptor. Here is the description St. John of the Cross gives of the contribution of the soul:

> "As the transformation in God depends neither on the senses nor on human skill, the soul must strip itself completely and *voluntarily* [our emphasis] of all which it might contain of affection for things high and low; the soul will do all that it can of itself; and then what will prevent God from acting freely in that humbled, stripped, annihilated soul?"

A little further on he says: "The soul must make every effort to know nothing . . . the soul must reduce all its imperfections to nothing."

These few lines, and other passages too numerous to be cited, describe the effort which the soul must put forth before being admitted to the passive stage. This degree is described thus in the *Bhagavad Gītā*: *sarvadharmān parityajya māmekam śaraṇam vraja.* Abandon all *dharmas* (duties) and take refuge in me only (XVIII, 66).

According to mystical theology, there are three degrees in spiritual life. The first, the *via purgativa*, describes the work which the soul must accomplish by itself; this stage is indicated in yoga by the terms *yama-niyama* (rules of mental discipline and purification); then comes the second degree, the *via contemplativa*, which in yoga corresponds to *pratyāhāra*, *dhāraṇā* and *dhyāna*; that is to say silent reflection, concentration, a state of contemplative meditation. The beginning of the *via contemplativa* involves a period of meditation, but, according to St. John of the Cross, discursive meditation soon gives way to infused contemplation; between the two there is an intermediary degree during which one cannot determine whether the soul acts or God is active in the soul; "so long as one has not arrived at that advanced state, there is a mixture of ways," writes St. John of the Cross. Discursive meditation corresponds to the practice of *pratyāhāra* and *dhāraṇā*; and when the aspirant arrives at *dhyāna*, he finds himself at the extreme limit of two states where one cannot distinguish between human action and the divine action infused in the soul. Sometimes it seems that the latter tries to attract God; sometimes it appears inactive and it seems as though God lets His grace flow into the heart of the disciple. We can read those descriptions in the litanies which the Vaiṣṇava saints have left us, such as the *via contemplativa* according to the method of yoga. The last stage of spiritual life, the *via unitiva*, is that of union with the divine; here, according to both Christian theology and Hindu method, it is God Himself who enters into union with the soul. From time to time, the Lord permits the soul to think that she still engages in some activity; but according to Hindu yoga, it is simply a matter of God's play. In the state of union, only the Lord acts, and His action is to possess the soul completely. According to the words of St. John of the Cross: "the soul becomes God by participation."

Misunderstandings with Western theologians always occur when they are presented with the problem of the annihilation of mental waves (*citta-vṛtti-nirodha*). In Yoga those whose interpretation of spiritual effort is limited to reducing mind to immobility are right to be pessimistic, for in itself, mental suicide proves nothing. Theologians, *yogīs*, philosophers, and metaphysicians who undertake the realization of the second *sūtra* of Patañjali do not see there an end in itself but a way of access to a correct view of Reality. The third *sūtra* is conceived thus: "Then [at the time of concentration] the seer [the *puruṣa*] resides in his own state [unmodified]." In this degree of concentration, all mental waves are suppressed; this state of annihilation is negative. The third *sūtra* describes the opposite, the positive aspect; any fact whatsoever has always two aspects: the positive and negative. If we plant a seed in the earth, it germinates. We can say that the skin of the seed has burst and is destroyed, or that the germ is born: the first statement is negative, the second positive. Between the two points of view there is temporal succession. There is no chronological relationship between the bursting of the skin and the germination of the plant. The event takes place in the eternity of the instant. Thus, there is no duration between the destruction of mental waves and the possession of the soul by the *puruṣa*. St. John of the Cross tells us that the resplendent sun appears on the horizon as soon as the third part of the Night is terminated.

In the metaphysical teaching of *Advaita*, the annihilation of mental waves has a definite purpose: it is a means which allows Reality to be apprehended. We habitually known only one aspect of Reality: the manifest aspect, expressed in consciousness by a series of perceptions; these perceptions, recorded by the mind as soon as they penetrated in the form of waves, are interpreted as actions. But that is only half of Reality; we are ignorant of the other aspect of the Real: SILENCE. Silence appears as soon as perceptions cease. The phenomenon of perceptions is possible, according to Hindu epistemology, only in relationship to its opposite, non-perception, which we experience in deep sleep. It is in contrasts and oppositions that life is felt as a living experience. SILENCE is what contradicts the movement of mental waves. Hindu metaphysics does not manifest any perference for one aspect over the other; but our mental activity presents us with a false vision of Reality. For *Vedānta*, as for Zen, clinging to opinions is the greatest obstacle to realization of the Supreme Doctrine. We must, at whatever cost, detach ourselves from life without, for all that attaching ourselves to SILENCE, to *SAMĀDHI*, the non-manifest aspect called, in the *Bṛhadāraṇyaka Upaniṣad*, death. Our preferences must go neither for life nor for death; it is only then that Reality unveils its secret in the realization of the Consciousness of *Turīya*. The discipline of Yoga is inevitable in order to make us grasp the importance of letting go, but this ultimate abandon occurs only when the most powerful of all our thoughts, the sense of "I," becomes detached from us. The greatest challenge we have to face is, according to St. John of the Cross, immersing the will into night, for the sense of the ego is attached to the will. We will take up this subject later. Here we will study only the night of understanding. We plan to treat the night of memory in a second section, and the night of will in a third.

The whole importance of the way of devotion is epitomized by the manner in which the disciple practices charity. For those who follow the metaphysical way (*jñāna*), annihilation of all thoughts recorded in the mental substance (*citta*) is particularly needful, for only that destruction will permit experiencing the interstitial void, namely, *samādhi*. *Satori** considered as an event seizes the disciple just at the moment when these two aspects of Reality, expression and non-expression, are placed on the same level simultaneously with the rising knowledge that the state of *jñāna* or *satori* has always been present. *Vedānta*, Zen, and St. John of the Cross unanimously affirm that no discipline will give the aspirant access to this final state. Vaiṣṇava schools categorically deny the efficacy of personal effort in the last phase of *sādhanā*, for it is accomplished only by the grace of the Lord in response to the total abandonment of the disciple. Advaitic metaphysics is not found in the yoga of St. John of the Cross, nor, for that matter, in Vaiṣṇava or Śhaivite teachings; for, no more than in the schools of Christian metaphysics, the extra-religious position is not considered. The teachings of St. John of the Cross remain circumscribed by the dogmas of the Holy Church, to which he affirms his complete submission. The faith of St. John of the Cross is the *Credo* of the Church: *God is a Trinity in persons and a Unity in nature*. The Vaiṣṇavite saints of India have a determined dogmatism from which they cannot depart. But the attitude imposed by the dogmas leaves us free to observe the full flowering of *Rāja-Yoga* in St. John of the Cross—*Rāja-Yoga* not allied with any theology whatsoever, although it exists as the most powerful moving force which propels us towards the realization of mystical theology, whatever our religions may be. Dogmas—Vaiṣṇava or Christian—enter in only when it becomes a matter of interpreting the *substance* of infused contemplation, for the actual fact of infused contemplation is never questioned by either Hindu or Christian schools. Our sole aim here is to interpret for our Western friends who are attracted to the Hindu approach the extraordinary fact which has fascinated us ever since we arrived in Europe: the discovery of Rāja-Yoga in St. John of the Cross. When visitors interested in India come to us and deplore, with a feeling of inferiority, that no equivalent for *Rāja-Yoga* exists in the tradition of the Occident, we advise them to read over and over and over the complete works of St. John of the Cross. We have done that ourselves, and we can say without any hesitation that we consider St. John of the Cross to be the Patañjali of the West.

2. CONTEMPLATION AND CHRISTIAN FAITH

Before continuing our study and establishing a parallel with the terminology of yoga, let us define clearly four terms used continually by St. John of the Cross: concentration, meditation, contemplation, and infused contemplation. We will take up the first three terms later. For the moment let us take up "Infused Contemplation" in the way the saint habitually uses it, and try to find its equilavent in the terms a *sādhaka* of yoga would use. Infused contemplation, according to St. John of the Cross, is the stage where the disciple abandons once and for all the initiative in his spiritual development. If we accept this definition, the Hindu term which corresponds to this conception will be *pratyakṣa* or *anubhava*, generally translated as "realization." It is what St. John of the Cross calls the "final term" which the soul discovers when she arrives at the end of her spiritual journey. This realization is accomplished by God in the human soul, but by pure convention we speak of the disciple's realization. The *Bhagavad Gītā* refers to this very clearly (IX, 47, 48) when Śrī Kṛṣṇa reveals his cosmic form to Arjuna: "I have granted you the boon, Arjuna, of seeing this supreme form revealed by my yoga." In the following *śloka*, the Lord specifies: "Neither sacrifice, nor the Vedas, nor alms, nor works, nor great austerity, nor deep study can bring forth the vision of this form." According to mystical theology, contemplation appears only after meditation has been abandoned. When the shadows of understanding, memory, and will have covered over the mind, announcing the dawn of the union of the soul with God; when the disciple has given up austerities and when a long series of successive humiliations has humbled his soul, humility is born of the knowledge that human efforts are powerless in this last stage of the evolution of the soul; after having gone through the active way, then the passive way—at that point contemplation begins, of which we have given the example of the vision Śrī Kṛṣṇa grants to Arjuna. Infused contemplation is the substance of the Christian faith: "God is a Trinity in Persons and a unity in nature"; it is the descent of God in man. This realization is accomplished by God; but man, in his ignorance, tries to appropriate it to himself by means of austerities, sacrifices, study, and other forms of spiritual practice. Likewise in the Advaitic tradition, the ego is extinguished in contemplation, the realization of the Eternal. Śaṁkara, in the verses which precede the text of the *Māṇḍūkyopaniṣad*, affirms without any possible equivocation, that Brahman Itself contemplates the universe in the states of waking (*jāgṛta*), dreams (*svapna*), and deep sleep (*suṣupti*), and he remains immutably identical to *turīya**(the intemporal). According to St. John of the Cross, man does not know the highest of all truths: God alone is, man appropriates to himself what legitimately belongs only to God. According to the words of Sri Ramakrishna, "God is in all men, but all men are not in God, which is the reason we suffer." St. John of the Cross, like the author of the *Bhagavad Gītā*, declares that this knowledge is given to man only by supernatural means, when the disciple practices *buddhi-yoga*, the yoga of discrimination, and the Lord gives him the gift of the "divine eye" (*divya cakṣu*).

According to the *Vedānta*, the Eternal is never limited by the manifestation contemplated by soul. When we use the term "unconditioned" in order to indicate what cannot be defined, we mean to give that term the sense of "absence of all conditions". Subjectively, we can suppress the conditions of the mind by stopping all mental movements, but that does not imply that the exterior world will cease to exist. When I go to sleep, the world does not at that time enter into silence. *Vedānta* and yoga are not to be equated with either subjective idealism or objective realism. The Real is expressed equally in either. The true sense of the Term "unconditioned" is the infinite possibility of all conditions. (According to the teachings of Sri Ramakrishna, divine forms are eternal—*nitya,* but are not a matter of the simple physical forms of Kṛṣṇa or Rāma). The illustration of clay enables us to grasp correctly this point of view. (We ask the reader to refer to the commentaries Śaṁkara has devoted to this question in the *Bṛhadāraṇyaka Upaniṣad,* pp. 17-22 in the Mayavati edition.) No one sees the clay independently of the forms which it takes; no one form is eternal. Each of the forms which pass successively before our vision is fashioned from clay; however, we cannot affirm that we see clay itself, since we cannot perceive the clay independently of the forms; we cannot, moreover, declare that we do not see the clay. We have a direct intuition of clay, and that intuition is unconditioned; but the forms are conditioned. Clay is endowed with infinite possibilities. Likewise the Eternal is never conditioned but possesses infinite possible ways of self-presentation. From the Vedāntic point of view, worshippers of the Eternal contemplate Him according to various religions, under a multiplicity of forms, which are so many revelations of the Eternal to men. From the esoteric point of view, these forms are presentations operated by *Puruṣa* itself when the substance of the Faith is revealed to a soul. The substance of Vaiṣṇava or Śaivite contemplations are not the same; thus we are justified in speaking equally of the substance of Christian faith; "God is a Trinity in Person and a Unity in nature." After having helped the disciple to pass through the dark Night by means of the trials of *citta-vṛtti-nirodha, Rāja Yoga* deposits him on the other shore, this time before a positive aspect: infused contemplation. In the course of this journey of transformation the soul has passed from the active state to the passive stage by the supernatural action of God's grace; or, putting it in Advaitic terms, she has arrived at the point where "Reality reveals itself." *Rāja-Yoga* does not experience the least difficulty in accepting Christian dogmas and considering them as numbered among the infinite possibilities which the Eternal uses in order to permit the disciple to contemplate Him.

With some trepidation we will try to establish the distinction between "contemplation" and "infused contemplation," as used by St. John of the Cross. The first designates that state in which the disciple "has that knowledge or loving view of God in a general manner." This stage is anterior to that of infused contemplation and posterior to discursive meditation; contemplative consciousness is knowledge identified with love, for which the Vedāntic equivalent, in Sanskrit, is *asti-bhāti* (existence-knowledge) or *sat-cit.* It is equally *priya* (or *ānanda*)—which is to say, love. This knowledge, or loving view, is identical with metaphysical intuition. Without having beforehand a firm intellectual conviction, our engagement in spiritual life will not be integral. Affective reactions change constantly, but intellectual convictions, born of *buddhi* (intellectual intuition) and sanctioned by it, are permanent, because, by workings of the *buddhi* we penetrate into universal regions. The particular is the field of emotional reactions, a veritable garden of errors; whereas intellectual intuition, the field of operation of the *buddhi*, becomes God by participation (to use the words of St. John of the Cross). The *buddhi* we are concerned with here is not the individual *buddhi* of the *antaḥkaraṇa* (internal organ), but the very light of the Eternal which strikes the *citta* (mental substance); and instead of letting the power of *māyā* project its multiplicity, this superior *buddhi* permits it to shine forth in all its glory. The inferior *buddhi* of the *antaḥkaraṇa* united to the *superior buddhi* constitutes the *mahat.** The intellectual truth contained in the Vedāntic formula "Thou art That" is the mainstay of students of *Vedānta*; but in dualistic traditions, intellectual conviction is just as necessary. In the Christian tradition, it is the moment when contemplation begins to intervene; let us read what the saint tells us about this knowledge or general view of God:

> For if the soul did not yet have this knowledge and this presence of God, it would follow that she would do nothing and know nothing; and, in fact, after having abandoned the meditation which helps her in discoursing through the senses, if contemplation was also missing, or the general knowledge we have spoken of—memory, understanding, and will, which are already united in that knowledge—she would necessarily be deprived of all use of it in relation to God; for the soul can neither act nor receive nor conserve what she has acquired, unless it be by means of these two powers (sense and spirit). . . . Hence it is necessary for her to possess that general

> knowledge before abandoning the way of meditation and resoning. . . . The soul neither sees nor feels the knowledge we speak of . . . . Thus the soul, lacking the knowledge furnished by understanding and the senses according to their usual capacities, no longer feels them. The soul no longer has her usual sensibility, . . . although this knowledge is purer, simpler, more perfect, it is less conscious and seems more obscure. . . . On the contrary, when the understanding of the soul is less pure and less simple, she seems clearer and more important; because when she is surrounded, combined, enveloped by intelligible forms, everything is more easily understood. . . . This general knowledge we are speaking of is communicated with so much purity and simplicity and at such a completely remote distance from all intelligible forms which are the usual objects of understanding, that the understanding is not even aware of it. Sometimes, when this knowledge is at its purest, the soul blinds the understanding because she deprives it of what usually illuminates—representation or images—and then it becomes aware of the darkness in which it finds itself.

The state of contemplation described above corresponds to the final stage of *dhyāna* according to the method of yoga: at that degree the mind is turned towards the Ideal which Faith incarnates. If we have followed attentively the reading of the work of St. John of the Cross, we will understand that in the word "Faith" is concentrated a great richness of meaning, capable of satisfying our heart and our mind at the same time. According to the interpretation of St. John of the Cross, Faith is the equivalent of the highest knowledge. Now we might profit by the occasion offered us here to make an observation on this matter. We often hear of people who have left the Catholic Church say that they have renounced Christianity because they could not find a rational, intellectual way of approaching it. For those people, the whole of Christianity is limited to devotion directed towards salvation. However, if we reflect on the idea of "general knowledge" the way the saint teaches it, as a necessary factor before abandoning meditation, we discover there a solid basis where the *buddhi* guides our approach to Reality. In our comparisons we must be fair and not take the best of our side to oppose the worst in our adversary's.

When we speak of a way of knowledge in the Christian tradition, we should take for our study those who, like St. John of the Cross, represent that way at its best, for whom the idea of faith is not merely an emotional dynamic but is also an arrow pointed towards the supreme Intelligence—which is another name for the Reality of God. For certain mystics, that method of approach is the awakening of pre-Adamic memories, an awakening provoked not by man but by the grace of God. That awakening cannot be obtained by intellectual or dialectical methods, since the intellect is vitiated by original sin. *Vedānta* would put it this way: the intellect dies into ignorance (*avidyā*) so that knowledge (*vidyā*) can rise out of a movement of ignorance.

Generally speaking, when we use the word "Faith," we are aware of our emotional reactions; but the meaning which St. John of the Cross gives this word corresponds to the Sanskrit *śraddhā*: etymologically *śrat* has the sense of Truth. Faith and Truth are thus synonyms. When we use the word "Truth," the reaction aroused in us has its source in our intelligence. We assert that, *in the yoga of St. John of the Cross, faith takes the place occupied by the "Iṣṭam" on which the disciple meditates, following the experiential way of yoga.* Faith and Christian revelation are identical, and we can say that these two terms are interchangeable; thus Jesus-Christ incarnates the Revelation. In the Hindu tradition, although at first the *Guru* and the *Iṣṭam* are conceived separately, at a given moment the disciple must realise the fusion of the *Guru* in the *Iṣṭam*, according to the way Sri Ramakrishna has explained it. Meditation on Jesus Christ is a meditation on Faith. The idea of Faith contains a dynamic charge of "intelligence", and it is what the saint suggests when he requires of the disciple "that general knowledge" destined to become—thanks to the knowledge of what must be done and what must be avoided—the structure of intelligence. St. John of the Cross witnesses to the same demand which the *Bhagavad Gītā* does: "Let these Scriptures be thus the authority which determines for you what must be done and what must not be done" (*BG*, XVI, 24). A deep intelligence is necessary to understand the Scriptures and to know how to find what must be done or avoided. Formal education is of no use here. Brother Lawrence, *Latu Mahārāj,* or Hui Neng* had no erudition. The intelligence we are speaking of is a free gift; as soon as it awakes in the soul—even in that of an illiterate—the mute become eloquent and the ignorant become erudite. St. John of the Cross considers that the disciple must possess that general knowledge before abandoning the way of meditation.

3. MEDITATION AND THE GURU

Next let us study St. John's concept of meditation. In the order of spiritual development, meditation is anterior to infused contemplation. Before getting into our subject, let us consider a question very important from the point of view of yoga: To what extent would St. John of the Cross accept the role of the Guru and the Iṣṭam? The Guru is a spiritual guide (for a guide is necessary in pursuing this difficult way). In entering the spiritual way, the disciple confronts a terrible ordeal, which consists of reducing his own individuality to nothing; the realization of the purpose is announced by the saint thus:

> The reader must also keep in mind the intention and the purpose I set myself in writing this book: my purpose was to direct the soul in all her natural and supernatural knowledge, freeing her from illusions and difficulties, in the purity of faith in order to attain union with the divine. (AMC, Bk, II, Ch. 28, 1)

Such are the actual words of St. John of the Cross. Beginning with his Prologue, he specifies that this road is very difficult, and that, in this work, he is not addressing the general public:

> Furthermore my main intention is not to address everyone in general but rather certain people, religious of the reform of Our Lady of Carmel. . . . God has given them the grace of setting them on the path of that mount. Since they are already totally stripped of the goods of this world, they will better understand this doctrine of spiritual nakedness. (Prologue, 9)

The doctrine of the Dark Night is not a practice within the reach of everyone.[1] It is reserved for those who have heard the call from

[1] "Since the doctrine applies to all those souls with spiritual practice, it is obvious one does not have to belong to a monastery to read these lines with profit. Nowadays the whole world is the monastery." Antonin T. de Nicholas, *St. John of the Cross*, p. 245.

the Lord: "Abandon all and follow me. . . . If someone wishes to follow my way, let him renounce, let him take up his cross and follow me. For whoever wishes to save his soul will lose it, and he who will lose it for love of me will save it" (Mark 8:34).

And St. John of the Cross cites from Genesis the story of Jacob climbing Mount Bethel in order to erect an altar and offer a sacrifice to God. (Gen. 35) Jacob imposed three conditions on those who would follow him: first, renounce foreign gods; second, purify yourself; third, change garments. The first condition implies renouncing all feelings related to anything or anyone other than God. The second is the purification by the Dark Night of the Soul, which is to say renunciation of all tendencies rooted in sensual attachment. The soul must mortify itself by a severe discipline; it must have the control of all sensual appetites and repent all past errors. The third condition, which consists of changing garments, means that the soul must be transformed. Human initiative is necessary for the first two conditions, but the third—changing garments—is the work of God. "God himself puts on the new garments. He endows the soul with a new faculty of knowing and loving God in himself." The disciple does not know how to put on these new garments. Here the help of the Guru is essential. The road travelled by the disciple is away from the flesh, according to the saint; it is a supernatural way, which leads to a different nature, transformed and transfigured. He preaches a monastic ideal. Here is a quotation from St. Paul taken from the end of Book III Chapter 18 of *AMC*:

> One thing is certain, my brothers: time is short; consequently let those who are married be as those who are not; those who weep be as those who do not; those who rejoice be as those who do not rejoice; let those who buy be as those who possess nothing; let those who deal with the world be as those who have no dealings with it. (I Cor. 7:29-31)

Only a sure guide can direct the soul towards its final destiny. Who is the Guru of Christians en route to perfection? The Holy Church. The Catholic Church is much more than an organization of the faithful, such as the *saṁgha* of the Buddhists; it is a higher idea. In fact, the Holy Church is considered the incarnation of faith, a living faith indicated by the feminine gender: one says "Our Mother Church." She is the mediator between the soul and

God. Her role is identical to the goddess in the Vaiṣṇavite tradition of Kṛṣṇa. It is interesting to establish a parallel between this idea of the Church and the Vaiṣṇavite notion of Kṛṣṇa as the Eternal Masculine and Rādhā the eternal Feminine. According to the Vaiṣṇavite tradition, the totality of the manifest (or created) world is *prakṛti*, which is to say, feminine. Let us make clear, however, that is no way a question of individual sex but a way of symbolizing positive and negative principles. The eternal non-transitory principle, *puruṣa*, is represented by the masculine, positive principle; whereas the Eternal Feminine represents the transitory (*prakṛti* or *māyā*), the negative principle. Let us note in passing the etymological sense of the word *māyā*: that which changes and never stays the same. Everything which belongs to *māyā* participates in its impermanent aspect; hence everything which belongs to this manifested world expresses the negative principle of change: all is feminine. This theory is that of the Vaiṣṇavite school of Śrī Kṛṣṇa Chaitanya. Liberation or mukti intervenes only at the moment when the faithful perceive the masculine principle, symbolized by Kṛṣṇa, as the Principle active in all things. The *jīva* (soul), submerged in ignorance, believes she is herself the agent, the author of her acts, whereas in reality only the eternal cosmic Principle works in each of us. How can one obtain that realization? It cannot be done except by the grace of Rādhā, the eternal feminine. The *gopīs* who surround Rādhā and Kṛṣṇa are souls. Each of them must be "transformed" into Rādhā, the eternal feminine, and for that contemplate herself in the mirror of Rādhā. Each of us one day will have to abandon the idea of being one who acts; there is a transposition in the teaching of St. John of the Cross when he urges us to submerge understanding, memory, and will in the Dark Night. The one who grants us mediation to help us reduce our personality to "nothing" — as St. John of the Cross puts it — is the Guru, the eternal feminine, and this is the role which the Church plays: the mediator. In Hindu mythology, the Eternal Feminine is incarnated by Rādhā or Lakṣmī or Sītā, whose proper grace metamorphosises each soul; each *gopī* is her proper form and attitude. In the Vaiṣṇavite tradition, this doctrine is called Śrī *Tattva*, or Lakṣmī *Tattva*. Thus the Mother-Church is the mediator between the soul and God; she plays the role of the Guru. The Holy Church is the Guru; the Holy Church is Faith. When the grace of the Guru is awakened in the heart of the disciple, the old man dies in him. We read in the *Gītā*: "What is night for all beings is the time of waking for the sage who sees; what is the time of waking all beings is night for the sage who sees." The Guru, the Church, awakes in us the sleeping creature. The powers of the soul are reduced to silence, faith comes to life, and the purified soul is united to the Eternal Masculine by the intermediary of the Eternal Feminine. In his book *On Love*, Dr. Benoit writes the following lines of the subject:

> In the ultimate time of realization, or intemporal realization, the triangle is otherwise constituted; the passive feminine pole is represented by the totality of the temporal aspect of man, with his "soma" and his "psyche"; the active masculine pole is the creative Principle which is at the centre of all created being, which is sometimes called "Spirit," in the sense in which this "Spirit" is anterior to the "body" and the "soul" at the same time. The spirit penetrates the psycho-somatic organism of the man, in an ultimate interior union, by virtue of a hypostasis which is then the very principle of Love, for which the scholastic term is "Agape" or the active role of the Supreme Principle for its passive creation. The result of that act of love is then the "new man," realized, "liberated," reunited to the Principle of all manifestation.

This guidance of the soul by the Holy Church is accomplished by means of Faith, which is expressed by possessing that general knowledge which contemplation furnishes. For *Rāja-Yoga*, one of the most essential practices is meditation on the Guru imagined in the heart of the disciple. In the work of St. John of the Cross, we do not find any special mention of meditation centered in that *cakra* (psychic centre), but the rigour imposed on the disciple for the purification of emotions, which constitutes the first part of the *via purgativa*, implies that a strict watch be kept over the impulses which precede our affectivity, which, according to popular belief, are seated in the heart. We know that the idea of abandoning meditation will shock our Hindu readers as well as those who have some familiarity with the directives usually given for Hindu meditation; for them, it would be difficult to admit that it is possible to give up the practice of meditation. Nevertheless, we will discover, in reading advanced Vaiṣṇavite texts, that a time comes when even meditation must be abandoned, since in meditation the soul is active, and activity comes from *ego*; thus, in a correct view of spirituality, work has no legitimate place. In fact, if the disciple has progressed, meditation on the Guru, or the Church and its doctrines, will have opened a way to contemplation, and meditation will cease of its own accord. But meditation, according to St. John of the Cross, will have served to create a new habit of love:

> Each time that the soul produces this fruit by meditation, she accomplishes an act . . . . and the multiplicity of acts finally will engender in the soul the habit, just as the multiple acts of knowledge full of Love of God which the soul produces to achieve the formation of habit . . . . He [God] sends them immediately into contemplation and into love. (*AMC*, 15, 15)

The acts the saint speaks of are called *kaiṅkarya* in the terminology of the Vaishnava saints of the school of *prabandha* in south India. St. John of the Cross adds that love establishes the resemblance between the one who loves and the beloved object. Love not only renders them similar but also subjects the one who loves to the beloved object. A long contact is necessary before love is born, says the saint, and meditation is the means of creating this habit. This is what the school of yoga calls *smaraṇa* and *manana* (memory and reflection): the current of meditation excites the soul to acts of love. There, where the soul takes up its abode, there lies our treasure. When the mind fastens itself to something which it does not possess but, on the contrary, the thing in question is what possesses it, then we are the slaves of our thoughts. How do we become the slaves of our thoughts of God? We must love Him, and that love comes only by dint of a habit formed by a constant association of our mind with the thought of God—what yoga calls *smaraṇa* and *manana*. If the Holy Church is the Guru, the disciple must obtain faith by constant meditation on the foundations of that faith. In order to interpret the function of the Guru without becoming enmeshed in what St. John of the Cross calls "a mass of errors and imperfections," the disciple must have recourse to the advice of a director of conscience. However, the director of conscience does not take the place of a Guru, and St. John of the Cross criticizes bitterly those directors of conscience who with time become a veritable danger for the spiritual evolution of the disciple; he exhorts disciples to find good directors of conscience.

Jesus Christ undoubtedly occupies the place occupied by the Iṣṭam in the yogic tradition. St. John of the Cross often repeats that "one makes progress only by imitating Christ; He is the way, the truth, the life. No one goes to the Father except by the Son, as He Himself proclaims" (*AMC*, Bk II, Ch. 7, 8).

This kind of meditation is analogous to that practised by students of Rāja-Yoga, who use images and visualizations. The saint describes in detail the snares and dangers this method presents; it risks leading the faithful away from the truth more than drawing them to it. In the course of a minute analysis, St. John of the Cross examines the dangers likely to divert the student from his purpose and turn him into a possessor of psychic and occult powers which the saint declares to be the work of demons. This is exactly the same temptation which lies in wait for those who follow certain practices of *Rāja-Yoga*; they risk falling into the clutches of powers (*siddhis*) which, naturally reinforce the ego instead of destroying it. Love for Christ is developed by following the way which he himself prepared for his disciples and not by embarking on an adventure which will yield him only supernatural powers. That way comes close to what Hindus call *mānasa pūjā*. Adoration and meditation begin with a kind of visualization of Kṛṣṇa, Rāma, or some other chosen ideal which the disciple imagines in his heart. According as the meditation develops, the centre of attention is displaced and glides from the physical form of the divinity into the faith which it represents. The mind is then submerged, so to speak, in that "general knowledge" to which the saint gives such great importance. The Lord Jesus (the *Iṣṭam*), the Faith, and that "general knowledge" fuse and become identical. For the students of yoga who practice *dhyāna*, the face of the ideal is identified with the contents of *praṇava* "*Oṃ*," the meaning of which is given in numerous Upaniṣads and their commentaries (e.g. the *Māṇḍūkya Upaniṣad*). The cosmic conception of that meditation is taught and transmitted only by initiation. Initiation is not a mysterious ritual; we use that term to indicate that it is a matter of knowledge which goes beyond the compass of public lecture and is transmitted individually. A psychoanalyst would say that a disciple is "qualified" only after having experienced transference. When the process of projection is completely terminated, at the end of his spiritual evolution, the disciple discovers that his *ātman* is the *sarvabhūtātmabhūtātma* (one whose Self is the Self of all loving beings): he is identical to that *ātman* which he had been worshipping. In the course of this process, love is born between the Guru and the disciple, an emotional bond which St. John of the Cross calls "betrothal" between the soul and God. This is the loving submission of the soul to the Church (or Guru). This is the moment when the disciple becomes the slave of the Guru, for St. John of the Cross teaches us that love not only makes the lover resemble the beloved object but subjects him to it. The term "Initiation" indicates a certain psychological maturity, since the riches of the Guru are transmitted to the disciple. The notion which we in India have of initiation in its most intensive form (not the ordinary rite by which each of us receives a *mantra* from the family Guru, *kula-guru*) is an interior awakening aroused by a real spiritual hunger. This kind of *dīkṣā* (initiation) is distinctly different from the initiation rites which bind one to a religious community, as for example, baptism for Christians or the investiture of the sacred thread (*upanayanam*) for Brahmins. The higher kind of initiation we want to discuss is found in the Bible. St. John of the Cross cites this passage:

> If there are among you certain prophets of the Lord, I will appear to them in dreams. But there is no one like my servant Moses; he is the most faithful in all the house. I speak to him mouth to mouth, and he sees the Lord not by means of comparisons, symbols, or images, but *Openly*. [italics added] (Num. 12:6-8)

This kind of initiation or realization is instantaneous and is accompanied by a transmission of knowledge. It is well-known in the history of Hindu mysticism, as when Sri Ramakrishna says to Swami Vivekananda, "I see God as I see you but in a manner much more intense," and at the initiation of the Swami by that vision Sri Ramakrishna used the same words of transmission, thanks to which the disciple sees the Lord, not by means of comparison, symbol, or image, but openly.

This meditation is not for everyone. In order to conquer the Faith St. John of the Cross speaks of, one must first pass through the *via purgativa*. Most members of a spiritual community indulge themselves in consolation. St. John of the Cross vehemently proves their error. All of us need compensations in life; those who wish to be free of the congenital need for compensation are rare. We try to replace the compensations of life with religious consolations. As we have already said, in the eyes of St. John of the Cross, Faith is knowledge, and in Knowledge there cannot be this personal factor which dominates our whole system of compensations. Very few of the Faithful reach the point where they see in Jesus Christ the incarnation of Faith which brings them the redemption of compensatory forces. St. John of the Cross makes no compromise when he writes:

> Jesus Christ is almost unknown to those who believe themselves his friends. We see them, in fact, seeking in him gentleness and consolation, see them loving themselves dearly, instead of seeking the bitterness and self-abasement which are the mark of the love they bear. As for those who live far from him and separated from him—the important people, scholars, potentates and others who live in the midst of the world, preoccupied with satisfying their ambitions and their desires for greatness—how can we say that they know not Christ? . . . . They are not dealt with in this writing. (*AMC.* Bk II, Ch. 7, 12)

The acquisition of general knowledge is identical to the acquisition of supernatural light. In his natural state, man identifies himself with the intelligible forms which are the proper object of understanding. The supernatural state, of which St. John of the Cross speaks, corresponds to the Vedāntic notion of *puruṣa* permitting the disciple to contemplate him, and we have already indicated on this subject that, according to the Hindu point of view, the possibilities of the Eternal are infinite. It is the teaching expounded in the *Bhagavad Gītā* IX, 15, where Reality is conceived in its unity, distinct from the soul, and as an omnipresent Multiplicity. A little further, in *slokas* 17 and 18 we read:

> I am the Father of the Universe, the Mother, the Sustainer, the Ancestor, the most Holy, which we must learn to know, the Word, the Power, and also the three Vedas. I am the Way, the Spouse, the Lord, the Witness, the Abode, the Refuge, the Lover, the Origin, the Dissolution, the Foundation, the Treasure, the Imperishable Seed.

For Christian Dogma, there is only one position, that which we have already cited: "God is a Trinity in Persons and a Unity in nature; this is how our Faith is presented to us." In the supernatural state, there is a complete disengagement and estrangement from all intelligible forms which are the proper objects of understanding, which the understanding does not feel nor see.... Sometimes even, when this knowledge is more pure, it blinds the understanding, because it deprives it of its natural light, its representations or images, and then it becomes aware of the shadows in which it finds itself.

From the point of view of understanding, the obscurity is complete, whereas from the point of view of knowledge all is light. For a study of the *Rāja-Yoga* of St. John of the Cross, the following passages are of the greatest importance:

> But when this light does not communicate to the soul with enough power, she perceives neither darkness nor light; she apprehends nothing of knowledge below nor on high; thus she finds herself sometimes, as it were, in an oblivion so profound that she knows neither where she is nor what she is doing; she is no longer aware of time passing.... And since this knowledge is pure and limpid, it makes the soul to whom it is communicating simple, pure, limpid, detached from all conceptions and memories of the senses or the mind. This knowledge will leave the soul behind, forgotten, outside any notion of time. Such is the *orison* which is said to penetrate heaven (Eccles. 35:21); it does not take place in time. It penetrates heaven because then the soul is united to God by its celestial intelligence; and when the soul awakens, she finds that this knowledge has left behind effects which she was not aware of, namely, the elevation of the mind to the intelligence of the things of God, detachment and estrangement from all terrestrial forms and shapes, and even the memory of them. (*AMC*, Bk II, Ch. 14, 10,11)

The descriptions of this *orison* corresponds, for a *yogī*, to a certain type of *savikalpa-samādhi* (state of union where duality still subsists).

In the same chapter, St. John of the Cross cites the sleep of the bride of the Song of Songs; one of the effects produced in her by sleep is oblivion, that is to say that state of absence due to Knowledge. She says then "*Nescivi*," "I do not know whence came that favour . . . ." Doubtless the harmony of the powers of the soul is suspended, but her intelligence is the state we described. That is why the Bride of the Song of Songs replies herself to resolve the difficulty: "*Ergo dormio, et cor meum vigilat*" (*SS*, 5:2). "Although I sleep according to my natural state (by ceasing to act) my heart is awake" because it has been elevated supernaturally to a supernatural knowledge. The proof by which one can know that the soul is occupied by this consists in the fact that she experiences no pleasure in created objects, inferior or superior. Let us pause a moment to recall sister Elizabeth of the Trinity* who, in our time, realized the sense of *Nescivi*. We do not wish to miss an occasion to establish the comparison between the state of the soul which sleeps while the heart is awake and these few lines from the *Vivekacūḍāmaṇi*:

> He whose mind is absorbed in Brahman—who is nevertheless always vigilant—who, at the same time, has shaken off all the characteristics of the waking state—we consider such a one a *jīvanmukta*.

We cite an Advaitic text, and the substance of the faith which it teaches is, certainly, different from that taught by the dualist systems; however, we have ascertained that all descriptions of realized souls have certain affinities. When the beginner notices that, according to those descriptions, the soul is not peacefully occupied in that knowledge, one will profit from discursive meditation. . . . When we say that the soul receives the light which is communicated supernaturally, we mean that she understands passively; when we say that she does not act, we do not mean that she does not understand; but she understands that which has cost no effort of personal diligence. When the moment has arrived and the soul leaves behind her personal diligence, if former tendencies return and urge her to take interest again in meditating on particular objects, that will be completely profitless and an obstacle to that general light of the spirit.

In this work, St. John of the Cross states a spiritual truth of the greatest importance for everyone:

> The man who has given himself to spiritual life, when he finds it difficult to meditate, must keep a firm and loving attention on God, and maintain tranquillity of mind, so that

> he meditates even when it seems to him that he is doing nothing. (*AMC*, Bk II, Ch. 15, 5)

St. John of the Cross gives valuable advice for that stage where discursive meditation leaves the soul:

> Let him be careful not to bring in thoughts about motives or images or reasoning in order not to disturb the soul and deprive it of the contentment and peace which she enjoys and throw her into repugnance and distaste. (*AMC*, Bk II. Ch. 15, 5)

To conclude Chapter XV of Book II, the saint quotes [paraphrases] these words of David:

> Learn to be empty of all things—inwardly and outwardly—and you will see that I am God. (Ps. 45:11)

4. THE DARK NIGHT OF THE SOUL

The Dark Night operates in three ways: Faith places understanding in the Night; Hope places memory in the Night; and Charity (or love) places will in the Night. St. John of the Cross can justly be considered one of the greatest *Rāja-Ygins*, for he discovered the way of immersing the three powers of the soul (Faith, Hope, and Charity). We have already stressed the importance of Christian Faith in the overall plan of St. John's Dark Night. As he understands it, Faith and the doctrine of Holy Church are one and the same thing. We have identified Holy Church with the Guru. Let us now try to go more deeply into what Faith means in his work. St. John of the Cross cites these words of St. Paul:

> Faith is a firm assurance of things we hope for, a demonstration of things we do not see. (Heb. II:1) Faith is the substance of things we hope for, and although understanding adheres to them with a firm certitude, they are not in the realm of things the understanding can discover; if they were, it would not be Faith. For, although Faith gives the understanding certitude, it does not give it clarity; on the contrary, Faith obscures understanding. (*AMC*, Bk II, Ch. 6, 2)

Faith cannot be revealed by understanding; its light does not shine in the soul before the understanding has been enshrouded by the Night. We have already seen that, for the yogī, this is the state where the mind is purged of its modifications (*vṛttis*). Here is what St. John of the Cross understands by firmly established faith:

> The intellect must, in order to be prepared for the divine union, be freed and purified of everything that pertains to the senses, stripped of all it can apprehend clearly, located in a deep calm, far from all natural activity — in a word, established in Faith. Faith alone is the proximate and proportionate means for the union of the soul with God; for the resemblance between the soul and God is so great that no other difference exists save that between seeing God and believing God. (*AMC*, Bk. II, Ch. 9 1)

Thus, faith is also a vision, found in the Hindu tradition when it speaks of the opening of the third eye. The understanding counts for nothing in this vision, which is awakened in the heart of the disciple by the grace of the Guru. According to St. John of the Cross, Holy Church and it alone grants this vision. The disciple must completely renounce any personal way of seeing. The Hindu tradition is equally intransigent: obedience to the Guru is absolutely essential. The words of Sri Ramakrishna, according to which one must test the Guru, apply only before he is accepted; the choice once made, submission is unconditional. The Catholic tradition does not have to deal with the difficulties which beset the Hindus in choosing a Guru, since the Church is the unique Guru, charged with the interpretation of the faith. Faith is heard by the ear. St. John of the Cross tells us that:

> Faith comes from hearing, and hearing is of the Word of Christ. (Romans 10:17) This is as though Paul were saying: Faith is not knowledge which is acquired through any of the senses; it enters through the ear. . . . Other kinds of knowledge are acquired by the light of the understanding: the knowledge of faith is acquired without that light; that light must even be sacrificed in order to keep the light of faith. If you do not believe, you will not understand (Isaiah 7:9) (*AMC*, Bk II, Ch. 3, 3, 4)

So faith springs from hearing, from *Śruti*. The *Bṛhadāraṇyaka Upaniṣad* teaches that the truth must first be heard, then reflected upon, and finally realized. The meditation recommended in the Upaniṣad is very similar to that taught by St. John of the Cross: for in neither of the two traditions can the Absolute become the object of thought. This meditation opens the way towards realization. St. John of the Cross often cites the Biblical affirmation of man's impossible situation with respect to seeing God: "Man cannot see and live." Let us recall the words of St. John of the Cross in which he identifies vision and faith: that vision, which has no connection with ordinary vision, consists in a super-intellectual apprehension of the substance of Faith; it remains completely independent of the working of the intellect.

We have already seen that Faith and knowledge are one and the same thing; hence that order of vision does not belong in any way to sensible experience. Let us cite once more these lines of St. John of the Cross: "Faith is the consent of the soul to what comes by hearing." The Revelation of Scripture is given to the disciple through the mouth of the Guru (Church); the disciple must be prepared to submit completely to the words he receives (*śruti*). The writings of Christian *śruti*—the substance of Faith as St. John of the Cross formulates it—is intuitive knowledge transmitted by words and received by the ear. Ears are superior to eyes. Eyes perceive forms; whoever lets himself be captured by forms falls into idolatry, whereas hearing provides knowledge. Only the speech of Scripture contains knowledge (*parāvidyā*); that superior knowledge has a universal character, is never polluted by idolatry, and is not within reach of just anyone. One of the specific traits of our *Kali-Yuga* is the attempt to democratize that knowledge—an ineffectual attempt, for that knowledge can never be obtained by the right to vote or universal suffrage. A certain maturity of comprehension is the first quality required; it is the fruit of the *via purgativa*. Purification of the mind transforms Faith into knowledge; then, according to St. John of the Cross, knowledge operates on the mind; it destroys the power of imagination and fantasy (*saṁkalpa* and *vikalpa*) and thereby devitalizes the mind; in other words, the purification of the mind in the course of discursive meditation destroys the faculty of projecting and imagining. If the process is handled correctly by an informed director of conscience, the power of the mind diminishes progressively; its field of action is reduced until it disappears altogether. To support his thesis, St. John of the Cross cites numerous Biblical texts, for instance David:

> He set darkness under His feet and He rose above the cherubim and flew upon the wings of the wind. He made darkness and the dark water His hiding place. (Ps. 18:10-12)

All that indicates the obscurity of faith. Then he cites Solomon: "The Lord promised to dwell in the dark cloud. Whenever God made solemn appearances, He showed Himself in a cloud. . . . (I Kings 8:12). There follows this citation from the book of Job: "God spoke to him from the heart of the whirlwind" (Job 38:1). This darkness symbolizes the obscurity of faith with which the divinity is clothed when communicating with the soul. God and faith are darkness and obscurity for our understanding.

The action of the Dark Night bears first of all on what St. John of the Cross calls "the two interior corporeal senses," namely imagination and fantasy, which yoga calls *saṁkalpa* and *vikalpa*. St. John of the Cross continues:

> The one produces a kind of imperfect reasoning; the other forms the image which conforms to the object represented.... Meditation is the work of these two faculties, since it is a discursive act built upon forms, figures and images fashioned by the senses, as when we imagine Christ crucified or bound to a column, or at one of the stations of the cross; or God seated on a throne in resplendent majesty; or when we imagine the glory of heaven to be an incomparable light, or picturing any other human or divine thing. Now the soul will have to cast out all these imaginings and leave the senses in darkness if she wishes to attain union with the divine. (*AMC*, Bk II, Ch. 12, 3)

Then, a little further on:

> Thus those who picture God in images, such as a devouring fire or a brilliant light or any other form, and think they have a good picture of Him are actually very far from Him. (*AMC*, Bk II, Ch. 12, 5)

Here we come to the matter of meditation and concentration,

a subject explored in great detail by *yogins.* Patañjali speaks of diverse objects of meditation which have as their purpose rendering the mind capable of intense concentration. The fifty-first *sūtra* of the first chapter explains the method of training for *samādhi* "without seed" (*nirbīja-samādhi*). The disciple does not touch his goal until he has destroyed any attachment to all categories of concentration and meditation. As soon as the control of *saṁkalpas* and *vikalpas* is complete, no kind of representation is any longer produced. St. John of the Cross accords permission ot use certain representations and meditations to those who are not yet initiated into a higher level of spiritual life. This is in order to:

> Enkindle bit by bit their love and feed their souls by means of the senses. But they must learn to do without representations and not stay at that stage; for if they did, they would never arrive at their goal, which has no connection with those means which have to be left behind. . . . Those means are like the steps of a staircase. They are only the means for climbing up. . . . We should not think that the Divine Being 'is like gold, or silver, or stone, a representation by art and imagination of man. (Acts 17:29, *AMC*, Bk II, Ch. 12, 5)

In this manner St. John of the Cross speaks to beginners who, after having used representations, become attached to them and do not try to go beyond them. They cry out in despair

> "If all this is only a means, where and when will we enjoy the goal?" Then the saint speaks of a degree to spiritual life during which they must apply themselves to discursive prayer by means of representations, images, forms, and figures (of which we have spoken); for we must not give them up sooner or later than the spirit requires. They must be left behind at just the right time so that they will not hinder the soul in her journey to God. It is equally necessary not to abandon imaginative meditation before the proper time, lest there be a regression. . . . For although the apprehensions of these faculties do not serve as proximate means of union for those who are not proficient, they serve nevertheless for beginners as a distant means for disposing and preparing their spirit; they serve equally to void their sense of all base material, worldly and natural forms of images. (*AMC*, Bk II, Ch. 13, 1)

All these remarks prove the depth of St. John's understanding of spiritual life. In India, the yogī uses the method of concentration and meditation to turn the mind away from worldly matters. Since the wandering mind cannot suspend its imagination and fantasies, at least he lets them have some sort of spiritual content. Śrī Ramaṇa Maharṣhi once told us this anecdote: the agitated and undisciplined mind can be compared with an elephant's trunk which is always in motion, breaking branch after branch of the tree to which he is attached. In order to prevent him from doing too much damage, a chain is put on his trunk. Immediately the animal begins to play with his chain. The same thing happens when imagination and fantasy are distracted by a spiritual subject. The movement of the elephant's trunk does not stop; its imagination is the same as before, but the subterfuge of the chain makes it possible to limit the damage.

St. John of the Cross gives a detailed description which indicates to the soul that the moment has come to abandon discursive meditation with its representations and images.

1. The soul finds that it has become impossible to meditate; one no longer finds pleasure or sweetness in meditating but only dryness.
2. The soul no longer experiences any wish to apply imagination or the senses to any exterior or interior object of meditation; not that the imaginative faculty ceases to functions, but that there is no longer any desire to apply it to those objects intentionally.
3. Our author tells us that the final signal is the most certain. "The soul finds pleasure in being alone with God in loving awareness of Him."

In this state the faculties (intellect, memory, will) are inactive; the soul enjoys an interior peace in that "general loving knowledge of God" of which we have already spoken (Summarised from *AMC*, Bk. II, Ch. 13, 2-4).

After having recognized these three signs simultaneously, the soul can quite safely abandon discursive meditation and enter into contemplation. However, St. John of the Cross insists that one must be careful here not to confuse tepidity and lack of concentration with the first sign. The soul must discover the second sign in herself, experiencing no desire to be concerned with anything other than God. But that is still not enough: she must be possessed by the desire to be alone with God. In fact, if the soul has no more inclination to meditate and experiences no attraction for anything else, "this state could proceed from melancholia or some other mood coming from the heart or the head, and the soul might let herself relax in the charm of that torpor." When these three signs are distinctly and simultaneously present in the soul, the soul discovers that the preliminary exercises in meditation were only "the shell of spiritual life."

At this point a particularly difficult stage of spiritual life begins. The man devoted to spiritual life holds firm in his loving attention to God and preserves peace in his mind when he cannot meditate; it even seems to him that he is doing nothing. The life of the disciple at this moment begins a long period of strong tension. Discursive meditation accompanied by images and representations no longer attracts him, but he has not yet reached infused contemplation. He has barely that general knowledge which we have studied already at great length.

The aspirant is protected from natural and supernatural dangers thanks to the discipline which Faith (the Church, the Guru) has imposed on him. One of the dangers which the *sādhak* meets on his way, yoga warns us, and which threatens to check his progress, is certainly the attraction which supernatural experiences can exert on his mind. How many people have we met, in India or in Europe, who know they have reached a very advanced state because they have visions! For St. John of the Cross their sole value is the following:

> When the soul is thus prepared by this natural exercise, God customarily enlightens and spiritualizes her further by some supernatural visions which we here call imaginary and which, as we have already said, produce a great fruition in the spirit, gradually raising her above grossness and very slowly perfecting her. (*AMC*, Bk II, Ch. 17, 4)

Here the help of the director of conscience becomes all important. He must establish beyond doubt which of the soul's experiences can rightly be accepted and which must be rejected. St. John of the Cross begins his explanation of this subject by considering some of the difficulties a director of conscience must confront in his relationship with the disciple. He says first of all,

"I understand how difficult it is to explain how the spirit of the disciple is formed in a secret and intimate manner of the model of his spiritual master. . . . One cannot explain anything concerning the disciple without explaining what concerns the master. Thus if the spiritual father is inclined towards visions, he cannot fail unconsciously to impress the same inclination onto his disciple," and if the disciple has the same inclination, he will hold the visions in all the greater esteem. When the confessor does not have the necessary prudence to turn his disciple away from those visions, he communicates the signs by which the good and bad visions are recognized and risks throwing the soul into all sorts of dangers and preoccupations. But there is more. Certain directors, noting that some souls are able to communicate with God, use them, asking them to reveal certain secrets; and those souls obey, thinking it licit to beg revelations in this way. If God harkens to their request, they become confident and imagine that God is happy about that— which is not true. Their acts and beliefs follow those revelations, and they become attached to that way of dealing with God. However, if it happens that the facts do not correspond to the revelations, they are amazed and ask themselves whether the revelations come from God or not, for according to them, the revelation would have to be realized the way they imagined it, "And that is a great illusion, for the revelations or Words of God do not always verify what men imagine." St. John of the Cross concludes by saying that God does not like that process, and He shows His irritation:

> What is certainly the best thing to do is to get those souls prudently to flee from such supernatural communications, and habituate them, as we have said, to seek purity in spiritual poverty and the darkness of faith, for that is the way which leads to union with God. (*AMC*, II, 27, 6)

In reading the following lines we think we hear an echo of Śaṁkara. St. John of the Cross tells us:

> For those who wish to follow our advice we propose accepting supernatural communications *if they conform to reason and to the teachings of the Gospel.* In that case, those communications are accepted, not because they come by revelation, but because they comform to reason, by leaving aside the question of revelation.

The prudence of St. John of the Cross is in perfect accord with the instructions we have received from the direct disciples of Srī Ramakrishna. Srī Śāradā Devī used to recommend to her spiritual children to keep their heads cool and their digestive system in good condition. If the brain heats up, it becomes easily subject to hallucinations. St. John of the Cross considers that even if the visions come from an authentic supernatural source, it is good to reject them and not accord them any importance. Instead of fortifying evangelical faith, visions remove the mind from the substance of Faith, for the substance of Faith surpasses all means of expression. Monks of a spiritual order have renounced their families, possessions, and worldly career for a single goal: to realize God. When under the pretext of spiritual experiences, they become subject to visions or supernatural voices, etc., with a few rare exceptions, the way is opened to schizophrenia or paranoia. Thus the Holy Mother says, with a kind of irony, that precisely those who have devoted their lives to a good cause (and their number is greater than one imagines), those whose prime objective is liberation (*mukti*) are the ones who get most tightly bound in the meshes of *māyā*. If the disciple finds a suitable spiritual director, those dangers are avoided; but often spiritual life is an evasion from the responsibilities of life, a search for artificial compensations and consolations which ends lamentably in pathological afflictions. St. John of the Cross fought fiercely against this kind of cheap spiritual glory. The saint's whole doctrine is completely oriented towards what Zen calls "letting go."[1] However, the supernatural forces which awaken in us are powerful claws which reinforce the grip of the ego instead of obliging it to let go.

5. IṢṬA AND INFUSED CONTEMPLATION

Let us pause a moment in our comparison of the traditional *Rāja-Yoga* of India and the Master Yogi of the Christian tradition: St. John of the Cross. Let us study the place and importance of an exercise assiduously practised by Hindu *Rāja-yogins*: *mānasa pūjā*. This exercise consists of the adoration of a mental image

[1]"Letting go" is discussed in chapter 21 of Benoit's *The Supreme Doctrine* (Swami's note).

accompanied by the repetition of a holy name. Swami Brahmananda (Sri Mahapurushji Maharaj), direct disciple of Sri Ramakrishna, used to advise us to meditate on a spiritual image or representation and synchronise *dhyāna* (concentration) with *japa*, or the repetition of the *mantra* received from the Guru. St. John of the Cross is of the contrary opinion. He recommends removing from the mind all its forms and images. How can we reconcile these two attitudes? The root of the contradiction is the metaphysical differences which condition the two spiritual viewpoints. Let us try to give an exact statement of the difference. The process of Christian realization, according to the Faith, is union with the divine, and proceeds by the elimination of all forms; St. John of the Cross gives a minute description of the nature of that union. The soul passes through ten degrees successively, nine of which are accessible on this earth; the tenth, the state of perfect union, is reserved for the soul's celestial glory after death.

Rāja-Yoga, as practised in India, teaches on the one hand, pure devotion (*bhakti*), which is the knowledge of the relationship between the soul and God, if the disciple belongs to a dualistic school; or if the disciple belongs to the Advaitic school, Advaitic knowledge which restores to man the memory of his identity with "that" (*tat tvam asi*): Thou art That. However, the teaching of *Rāja-Yoga* also includes a knowledge of the totality (*sarvam*). The totality is time and space. The compass of all manifestation (time, space, causality) constitutes *māyā*. The Christian idea is to strive to attain a state of transcendence beyond time, or at least a state where time is arrested. The aim of *Rāja-Yoga* in India consists of suppressing all modifications of the mind in order to attain *samādhi* without seed; this process corresponds to the immersion of the mind in the Dark Night. For us, that experience brings knowledge of only half of Reality—if indeed we can use that expression; the other half is *māyā*, the manifest world. The disciple now strives to obtain knowledge of *māyā*, instead of being satisfied with rejecting it as an obstacle. Our understanding is limited by our ignorance, which engenders ignorance in turn, and precludes a "synoptic" view of Reality; thus the characteristic of ignorance is a partial vision of *māyā*, and, according to the *śākta* school, *māyā* is assimilated into the *śākti* (energy) of Brahman, which is to say, Reality. This limited vision of ignorance stirs up false identification (*adhyāsa*) and makes us take the part for the whole. As soon as we have acknowledged that *knowledge of māyā is Brahman,* we know the there is no difference between the Absolute and its manifestation. This is the concept of *sarvam,* and, since the Totality is identical with the *Sakti* of Brahman, that is the same as to say that the Totality is Brahman (*sarvam khalvidam brahma*). This is the summit of the Vedāntic teaching to which *Rāja-Yoga* leads us.

The temporary thesis which *Vedānta* lays down at the beginning of spiritual life is this : *brahman satyam, jagad mithyā,* Brahman is the Reality, the world is illusion; and it terminates in the ultimate truth of spiritual life; *sarvam khalvidam brahma,* the totality (*Sakti*) is Brahman. Now let us take a look at the road which *Vedānta* takes before achieving that result. In order to school the disciple in concentration (*dhyāna*), he is asked to fix his mind on an image or a fixed object, and to repeat simultaneously a *mantram* (sacred formula). We are going to explain the profound metaphysical singnificance of this kind of *dhyāna.* The fixed object symbolizes the idea of space.[1] The original notion of space is awakened in us by some landmark, some fixed object. For instance, the sun or a whole celestial constellation. The first experience is cognized as the distance between two fixed points, but we quickly note that a single point (the Sun) itself consists of space (*diśa* or *ākāśa*). The bricks with which a wall is constructed appear separated in space; but in fact, they are themselves only a condensation of space. The eminent professor Theodore Kārmān*, an authority on aerodynamics, explained to us that according to modern science, matter is nothing but a condensation of empty space. We think that it is possible to find a connection between that scientific view and the Vedāntic cosmology; the *ākāśa* of *Vedānta* is "empty space" and *prāṇa* (the primordial energy or *śakti*) is a condensation of *ākāśa.*[2] In Art, the metaphysical concept is expressed by the dance of Kālī. The divine *śakti* (primordial energy) dances on the motionless body of Śiva, her spouse, the Immutable, the Absolute. Her dance is time in its multiple manifestations, and it projects

---

[1]On this subject see *The World as Power: Power as Consciousness* by S. J. Woodroffe* (Swami's note).

[2]See in *Hommes et Mondes,* September 1952, an article by Lincoln Barnett on the physicist Oppenheimer, whose "interest in Oriental thought is based on analogies between Hindu philosophy and philosophical ideas developed by modern science" (Swami's note).

all the worlds. The entire universe is nothing other than an expression of *prāṇa*, a condensation of *ākāśa*, empty space, simultaneously conceived as ultimate Reality. *Prāṇa* is the totality of the manifested universe. "Beings are non-manifested in their origin, manifested in their intermediary state, O Bhārata, and non-manifested in their dissolution" (*BG*, II, 28). The totality of that manifested universe is Vāsudeva: "A condensation of the Absolute."... if it is possible to juxtapose thus two radically contradictory notions.

Now we are going to see by what process Vedāntic thought arrives at the knowledge of *ākāśa*, the source and origin of all existence, which penetrates everything. The method of meditation in *Rāja-Yoga* uses certain symbols (*pratīkas*). As concentration intensifies, the object of meditation loses its particular form; it expands in the field of consciousness of the meditator, and by that expansion the meditator penetrates ever more subtle states (*cittākāśa*). Attachment to a determined form to the exclusion of all others is idolatry. Here we can refer again to the illustration of clay seen as prime matter; the capacity to conceive an infinity of possible forms in the clay is equivalent to the Cosmic form, the matrix of all forms, in the essence of which all forms find their mould. Attraction towards fixed Reality in a unique form to the exclusion of all other forms proceeds from the desire for compensation and results from false identification. Our friend Dr. H. Benoit* has written a very interesting page on that question:

> Our compensations are necessary to our total realization since without them we could not accept existence, and we would destroy ourselves at once; they are on the way of our correct evolution towards *satori*. But the obtaining of *satori* assumes that some day we shall pass beyond our compensations. This passing-beyond should be understood not as a loss of the vivifying substance contained in our compensations, but as a bursting of the formal and exclusive circumference which was limiting this substance. The reality seen in the idol is not wiped out but is diffused outside the idol whose restrictive circumference has burst. (Hubert Benoit, *The Supreme Doctrine*, p. 212)

The *Bhāgavat Purāṇa* recommends urgently to its students that they practise this form of meditation of which Kṛṣṇa is the classical symbol. The iṣṭa—the Ideal—progressively loses its spatial character, its particularized aspect, its physical, human traits; its personal history disappears; it becomes the Infinite; it becomes Consciousness.

Different states of matter, the four elements, must have a common milieu. First of all, and in order to accommodate an hierarchical order, one attributes this character to thought, and one conceives the *ākāśa* as a separate base, a fifth element, from which the four others derive their existence. When comprehension attains a certain maturity, the idea of a container and a content vanish, abandoned as a last vestige of ignorance; one realizes the identity of the two factors. Finally, the very notion of a common milieu disappears. This position joins current conceptions of science: *ākāśa* and pure Consciousness are identical: *caitanya* in *Vedānta*; *śūnyatā* or *tatathā* (thatness) in Mahāyāna Buddhism. Three aspects of *ākāśa* are distinguished, which correspond respectively to the gross or physical state: *mahākāśa*; the subtle state: *cittākāśa*; and the causal or seminal state: *cidākāśa*. The dream state, enables us to realize that all is consciousness: "In the dream state, when contact with the exterior world is momentarily cut off, without any outside help, the mind creates different elements which compose the complete universe. But that is what is created equally while awake. Between these two conditions there is not the slightest difference. Consequently, the whole empirical universe is only the product of the Cosmic Mind" (*Vivekacūḍāmaṇi*, v. 170). Looked at from the angle of causality, *ākāśa* is the source from which other states of inert matter (*jaḍa*) are born; looked at from the extra-causal angle, *ākāśa* is then consciousness, and matter, energy (or *prāṇa*) is also consciousness. In Vedāntic terminology, the object is called *viṣaya caitanya*, which is to say, matter seized as an expression or condensation of Consciousness. Thus the entire world is Thought (that term is for us synonymous with consciousness). (The conception is very close to that of Sir James Jeans* in *The Mysterious Universe*.) We see now that meditation on a chosen ideal used as a fixed symbol permits us, by the expansion of the image, to attain to the Cosmic Form. The cosmos (*virāṭ*) in turn becomes one with *Īśvara* as the invocation to the *Māṇḍūkyopaniṣad* teaches us: *Virāṭ* (the gross, physical, sensible world) is Brahman.

We are now in a position to appreciate the metaphysical

significance of a form of meditation which, by means of concentration on an image—an idol—makes use of that image to destroy idols. The image is not *mṛnmayī*, "constituted clay," but in fact it is, according to the words of Sri Ramakrishna, *cinmayī*, condensation of Consciousness.

If meditation on the Iṣṭam which one uses as the centre of concentration or a fixed point has such an importance and leads us to metaphysical illumination, the repetition of the *mantra* leads us to the same realization, in this case by comprehending the process of Time.

The foundation of our experience of space rests on a fixed point; however, the notion of fixity is itself possible only by relating it to the opposite factor: movement (or psychological time). We become conscious of duration by the succession of thoughts, just as our notion of objective (chronological) time is a consequence of the course of the sun in the sky. Since our object of meditation, the *Iṣṭam*, has absorbed the total value of space, let us accord a parallel infinite value to the thought formulated in the *mantram*. Our intellectual way of doing things makes an artificial division of Reality into time and space, but it is an indivisible Totality. This is how the web of *māyā* is spun. Thought is consciousness, but a thought or an idea becomes a source of ignorance as soon as it excludes all other thoughts in the same way as attachment to an object or a form is a pit of errors as soon as it excludes all other objects. We eliminate the error or an object when we perceive in it the prime matter of which it is only a presentation, and thereby we perceive simultaneously in it the possibility of all other objects. In parallel we eliminate ignorance of a thought in apprehending through it the prime matter of which it formulates a particular presentation and by seizing in it simultaneously possibility of all other thoughts. This unique idea, whose force condenses into itself, becomes the focal point of all other thoughts: the *mantram*. The first part of meditation was applied to space. We took, for our point of departure, matter and its different states, and we arrived at Consciousness. In meditating on a *mantram*, the order is reversed: beginning with the production of sound, a specific property of the *ākāśka* (according to the teachings of *tantra* and *sāṁkhya*), we attend the birth, or rather the projection, of the other elements, by the "degradation" of consciousness into matter; the *ākāśa* or consciousness), by condensing itself into *prāṇa*, is degraded. If we envisage now the articulation of the *mantra*, as consciouness and the basis of "Reality," we will embrace the totality of the manifest world in descending order; whereas by meditating on a form or image, we are present for the reintegration of the elements in the ascending order, following a lightening of the more and more subtle *prāṇa* of which they are constituted, until they are fused in the *ākāśa*. Thus, the Hindu way of *Rāja-Yoga* leads the disciple to contemplation and to infused contemplation according to a way of approach which would not agree with Christianity. However, in the course of a conversation at Strasbourg with Dr. Albert Schweitzer,* we heard him mention a Christian cosmic approach. The cosmogonic conceptions are very different in the Hindu and the Judeo-Christian traditions; in my opinion, it is an error to mix them in order to try to see a unity where the modes of approach differ. While practicing *dhyāna* the disciple learns by synchronizing his visual contemplation of the *iṣṭa* with the sound of the *mantra*. This is something impossible to obtain by discipline, in fact; the discipline is a *method*. The mind can follow a method only when it is in the field of opposing currents. In the course of meditation on the *iṣṭa*, the chosen Ideal, represents the totality of the manifest universe. The meditator begins with the elements and reascends to the earth, water, fire, the air,[1] until his meditation leads him to the very source of those elements, the *ākāśa*, whose nature is consciousness. Simultaneously, meditation on the *mantra* reverses evolution; *śabda* (sound) is the specific property of the *ākāśa*, itself identical to *cidākāśa*, or pure consciousness. The primordial vibration (*nāda*) is rendered concrete in a point (*bindu*). That point is a *tension*, at the same time the cause and the result of the concentration of the waves of vibration. This is why the *bindu* is simultaneously the point of the disintegration of matter and the origin of its multiple states. These two processes, ascending and descending (*anuloma* and *pratiloma*), otherwise called cosmic evolution and involution, are synchronized in Attention (Capital "A"); the former is awakened at the ultimate realization—the *satori** event. The tension which engenders the power of attention (function of the

---

[1]The study of the elements according to an ascending order is nothing but the study of the solid, liquid, igneous, and gaseous states of mater which are expressions of energy or prāṇa (The Swami's note).

mind) makes it burst forth. The vast conception is comparable to the thought of the Zen writer, Professor Suzuki,* who said that *The universe is the greatest of Koans.* The response to that *Koan,* to that "brain-racker," cannot be furnished by the attention the mind might give to it, however sharp the mind might be, because attention has its pivot-point in the *ego.* Consequently, the particular attention whose reality is of the temporal order must give place to the objectless attention, that is non-temporal Attention [See Benoit's *The Supreme Doctrine,* Chapter 19] which one can represent symbolically by a fixed and empty look [See Suzuki's *The Zen Doctrine of No-Mind*] like that of a bird brooding, to use Sri Ramakrishna's illustration. At this point of the *sādhanā,* where the tension attains its maximum intensity, the "letting go" operates and the disciple realizes the truth of the verse from the *Gītā* already quoted: "Leave all duty, take refuge in me" (XVIII, 66). This is *saraṇāgati;* this is he realization of *samadhi.*

The etymology of the word *samādhi* would be of interest here; the prefix *sam* signifies "completely," *a* indicates the return towards the subject, and *dha* has the sense of maintaining together; *samadhi* is the substantive of the verb *samādhi*: to assemble completely. In the state of *samādhi,* the tension borne between two poles of existence (object and thought) is reduced to zero. The bifurcation of Reality into two apparent poles releases a wave of dispersed energy (*prāṇa*) which is diffused into a projection of the cosmos. As soon as this dispersion is re-integrated into its previous homogeneous and concentrated state, it is Unity (*puruṣa*) Concentration is thus the intermediary stage between meditation and contemplation, according to the terminology of St. John of the Cross. Concentration (*dhāraṇā*) itself has been preceded by *pratyāhāra,* the act of fixing the attention in order to sharpen it (*ekāgra*).

The disciple has acquired a correct understanding by his general knowledge and metaphysical intuition; he knows that the duality created by time and space (or the object and thought) is purely artificial.

That correct understanding, the goal of contemplation, will never reach maturity so long as it remains an ideal to be attained by effort (*sādhanā*), since the pivot-point of the effort is a modification of the imagination (*saṁkalpa*) of the disciple; so long as the *saṁkalpa* will not agree to "let go," illumination will remain impossible. "Know, O Pāṇḍava, that that which is called renunciation is truly yoga. He who has not renounced imagination and desire cannot become a yogī" (*BG*, VI, 2). At that stage, the contraction of the third eye is very strong; the more the disciple exerts himself, the more the third eye contracts. The final relaxation will be produced only in the moment when Reality will come to us; we will then experience infused contemplation or, as we called it at the beginning of this article, *pratyakṣānubhava*, that is to say, direct experience. "*Mukto hobé kobé ami jabé jobé*," the Bengali sentence spoken by Sri Ramakrishna, means: "As soon as the "I" disappears, the lightning of liberation will flash."

India does not know any fixed dogma regarding infused contemplation, no special commandment from the Lord as to the particular form by which He reveals Himself, unlike Catholic dogma, according to which "God is a Trinity in Persons and a Unity in Nature." It would be easy to identify in the work of St. John of the Cross other degrees of *aṣṭāṅga-yoga* which we have not mentioned, but that would take us beyond the scope of an article, and that is why we have limited ourselves to the principle phases of yoga: *dhyāna*, *dhāraṇā* and *pratyāhāra*; for the same reason we have decided not to give more quotations related to those terms. The reader is now in a position to understand why objections formulated by St. John of the Cross in regard to meditation on an image cannot be applied to the *sādhanā* of Hindu *Rāja-Yoga*. In contrast to St. John of the Cross, for us the image occupies an important place in the overall plan of *Rāja-Yoga*. The reason for this divergence lies in our different points of view.

The repetition of "Our Father," such as St. John of the Cross recommends, cannot be compared to meditation by the yogi on a *mantram*. For the disciple, the sacred *mantram* is identical to the divine presence. Just as the Catholic does not consider the bread and wine of the Eucharist to be symbols, so the Hindu disciple does not consider the *mantram* to be a symbol. The Hindu tradition teaches us that after the consecration of the *mantram* by the guru, the *mantram* takes on the splendour of pure Consciousness (*caitanya*). The repetition of the Jesus prayer in the Byzantine tradition is an echo of the practice of the *mantram*, without, nevertheless, having the same basis as in the Hindu tradition. (See *The Way of a Pilgrim* and the *Philocalia*. Readers particularly interested in these questions can profitably study the writings of

Sir John Woodroffe.) Contemplating an object, the *iṣṭa*, synchronized with the contemplation of the *mantram* in *japa* (repetition), leads to a total realization. The following illustration will clarify what we mean by "synchronization."

When we look at an image in a stereoscope, the vision of the right eye and that of the left eye takes place at the same level, which gives the sense of depth, of a third dimension, which is not one composed of two visions. It is not a synthesis; it is a new vision. In the same way we envisage the synchronization of time and space. This new vision is the opening of the third eye, the Vision of *māyā* considered as Reality, the Realization that All is Brahman. That is what *Vedānta* calls Liberation. All that we have seen up to this point, is nothing other than ways, modalities, for expressing Brahman.

Beginning with that instant the intellect ceases to divide and fragment Reality into objects and thoughts, into time and space, since in the Truth, dualism despite its fundamental appearances, does not exist. Before obtaining that direct experience (*sākṣātkāra*), the disciple goes through a preparatory stage in order to purify his thoughts and reflections. He must liberate his intelligence and keep it safe from the expropriation of his intellect. One might say of intelligence that it is cosmic, in the sense that it is endowed with infinite possibilities: of representation in the *citta* (mental substance), and of intellectual activity, for the intellect is one of its functions.

Liberation is the authentification of the cosmic character of the mind; henceforth the individual mind is no longer imprisoned nor limited by a personal point of view. That liberty of the mind, which will never let itself be bound by opinions, which will no longer cherish opinions, as Zen puts is, or, for *Vedānta,* will not be a prisoner of *mata* (opinion)—that liberty is a realization of *tattva,* Reality. The intellect considered as a "granary of opinions" is destroyed by this knowledge; it abandons definitively its beliefs; it is delivered from all particular attention which crystallizes around the illusory "I." The result, according to Saṁkara, is the experience of Brahman. The apparent contradiction between the futility of human effort and the final realization is resolved by one word: Grace.

The Hindu way of infused contemplation, like the philosophy and the metaphysics which govern it, is inadmissible for Christians.

St. John of the Cross says quite clearly:

> We should seek not to attach our hearts to rites or manners of praying which differ from what Christ and his Church have taught us. . . . We should not use other manners of prayer, formulas, or equivocal affectations, but we should follow only the prayers of the Church with the rite which the Church uses; everything else can be reduced to the Lord's Prayer. (*AMC*, Bk, III, Ch. 44, 4)

6. INTEGRAL YOGA

We have established that there are similarities and differences between the yoga of St. John of the Cross and the classical *Rāja-Yoga* of India, but our presentation has followed an order which reverses the traditional one. Usually an explanation of *Rāja-Yoga* follows an asending order: *Yama* (rules of discipline), *niyama* (purification), *pratyāhāra* (meditation), *dhāraṇā* (concentration), *dhyāna* (contemplation), *samādhi* (infused contemplation).

We studied *samādhi* first, which corresponds to the infused contemplation of St. John of the Cross, and in descending order we undertook the study of the other branches (*aṅgas*) of yoga. We have yet to treat *prāṇāyāma, āsana, niyama,* and *yama.*

The latter two have been largely dealt with in describing the Night of the Senses. St. John of the Cross does not mention anywhere the practice of *prāṇāyāma.* In order to find a parallel for Indian *prāṇāyāma* in the Christian tradition, our researches would have to take us to Ignace de Loyola. As far as *āsana* (posture) is concerned, St. John of the Cross gives some direction about the choice of a solitary place for prayer, but without prescribing the gymnastics that Hindu *Rāja-Yoga* borrowed from *Haṭha-Yoga.* For him it is all simple and uncomplicated.

One of the fundamental principles required by St. John of the Cross as well as by Hindu *Rāja-Yoga* is the absolute observance of chastity; that rule, which does not allow any derogation, immediately eliminates a certain number of aspirants. We have cited the words of St. Paul to which St. John of the Cross refers: "One thing is certain, my brothers: the time is short; consequently, let those who are married be as those who are not" (I Cor. 7:29). *Rāja-Yoga* studies the question of chastity from the point of view of dispersion and concentration of energy; St. John of the Cross observes the same attitude.

> For God has so thoroughly weaned the soul from all its appetites, he has so well recollected them in Him, that they can no longer find any satisfaction in what they used to like. The end that God pursues in separating them from everything else and centering them in Him is to make the soul stronger and more fit to receive the strong union of God's love, which He is now beginning to give through this Purgative Way, in which the soul must love with great strength and with all her desires of both spirit and sense; which could not happen if they were dispersed in diverse other things. For this reason David said to God, to the end that he might receive the strength of this union with God, 'I will keep my strength for Thee' (Ps. 58:10). That is, all the ability, appetites, and strength of my faculties. I do not desire to make use of them or find satisfaction in anything outside of you.(*DN*, Bk II, Ch. 11, 3)

Conserving strength, in the concrete and subtle sense, is called *brahmacarya* in Hindu. We read in the *Bhagavad Gītā*, "I am going to reveal to you briefly the way which those who know the Vedas declare to be indestructible, which those follow who are masters of themselves, free from all passion; that way which one cannot take without taking the vow of chastity." It is impossible to undertake a spiritual discipline leading to *samādhi* without that observance. Furthermore, the etymology of the term, *samādhi*, which we pointed out above, is itself revealing: to hold together, to reassemble what is dispersed. This dispersion exists equally with the intellect, the memory, and the will. The role of active work which the soul must accomplish in order to penetrate into the Night was explained at the beginning of this essay, and, according to St. John of the Cross, as soon as the soul has done her part of "personal industry," namely witnessing the creature's love for God, God places the soul in a passive state which makes it qualified to contemplate Him in His eternal glory in a state of complete union.

7. CONCLUSION

Here we find the tenth and last rung of love of this secret ladder. The soul is wholly assimilated to God as a consequence of the clear vision of God which she enjoys immediately. When the soul arrives at the ninth rung, nothing remains but to abandon her body. Souls like this are few in number; as love has worked a complete purification in them, they do not go through purgatory. That is why St. Matthew said, "Blessed are the pure in heart, for they will see God" (Mt. 5:8). Now, as we just said, this vision explains the total similarity of the soul with God, according to the saying of St. John: "We know that we will be like him" (Jn. 3:2). That does not mean that the soul will be as powerful as God, for that is impossible; but all that the soul is will become like God; thus she could be called, and in reality would be, God by participation:

> On that day you will not ask me anything (Jn. 16:23). But until that day arrives, there is always for the soul, however elevated she might be, something hidden in proportion to her lack of total assimilation to the divine essence. (*DN*, Bk. II, Ch. 20, 6)

This devotional result (*bhakti*) of *Rāja-Yoga* is the favourite theme of Hindu mystics. The different degrees are useful so long as the soul is not embraced by what St. John of the Cross calls "the fire of love." The *bhakti* school of India mentions some extremely rare cases where divine love seized a soul enmeshed in sin, and without passing her through the different stages of discipline, brusquely placed her at the highest summit of perfection. Here St. John of the Cross tells us:

> Here is the way this mystical theology and this secret love raise the soul above all created things and mount up, striving to reach the centre of its sphere." (*DN*, Bk II, Ch. 20, 6)

At this point, whatever differences there might be between one yoga and the other escape us. Furthermore, the yoga of St. John of the Cross is not limited to one of the four yogas *jñāna*, *bhakti*, *karma, rāja*—to the exclusion of others, but is integrates all four. In this sense, one could name it "integral yoga," (or *Pūrṇa Yoga*, the term used by Sri Aurobindo). Among the Christian mystics, to whom in one way or another we can apply the term Yogī, St. John of the Cross can be called the yogī *par excellence*, because in him alone do we find all the elements of different yogas harmonised by the supremacy of Christian faith.

In concluding this essay on the *Rāja-Yoga* of St. John of the Cross, we wish to pay homage to that distant period of history when the Orient and the Occident entered into intimate relations by a way which we have been unaware of for a long time.[1] When Plato accompanied the expedition of the Emperor Gordin to the Orient, he took a lively interest in the philosophy and spiritual practices of Persia and India and gathered information about them. Then in the fourth and fifth centuries C.E., by the intermediary of the neo-Platonists and other channels, the most precious elements of Hindu thought penetrated Christianity and were integrated into the body of Christian mysticism. St. Augustine played an important role in this work of assimilation. But the most important work of diffusion and assimlation was accomplished by a Syrian monk who chose to remain anonymous in order that his work might be more widely read. He was known under the pseudonym of Dionysius the Aeropagite. His two works, *The Divine Names* and *Mystical Theology*, won great popularity. The author presents the mystical tradition in a form more severe than the most ascetic *Vedātin* could ever imagine. Translated in the ninth century by John Scotus Erigena, these works enjoyed great popularity, and during the whole of the Middle Ages exercised considerable influence on all those devoted to meditation and contemplation. In the fourteenth century there appeared in England a work entitled *The Cloud of Unknowing*. In this small volume, which made a great impression when it appeared in England and all Europe, we find the development of Dionysian mysticism and of all its essential characteristics. Let us finish by citing the opinion of Fr. John Chapman on this book. He says, "It seems to sum up in advance the doctrines of St. John of the Cross."

---

[1] In this last paragraph, the author sums up the ideas of Aldous Huxley in Chapter 3 of his *Grey Eminence*. (author's note)

Notes on Persons and Books

Adbhutānanda (d. 1920): An orphan and a servant of one of Sri Ramakrishna's devotees. Sri Ramakrishna called him Latu. He was the only one of the direct disciples who was completely uneducated.

Benoit, Dr. Hubert: French Freudian psychiatrist and student of Zen. A lifelong friend of Swami Siddheswarananda. The Swami wrote a twelve-page preface to his *La Doctrine Suprême selon la Pensée Zen* (1951), in which he claims an importance for the book equal to that of Bergon's *Creative Evolution.* The English edition (*The Supreme Doctrine: Psychological Studies in Zen Thought,* 1955) does not include the Swami's preface but has a foreword by Aldous Huxley. The Swami also wrote a short preface to *Lacher et Prise: Théorie et Pratique selon le Zen* (3rd edition, 1971) (English edition: *Let Go! Theory and Practice of Detachment According to Zen,* 1962). Dr. Benoit says this volume completes the thought of *The Supreme Doctrine.* The Swami also refers to *De L'Amour, Psychologie de la vie Affective et Sexuelle* (1952) (*The Many Faces of Love: the Psychology of the Emotional and Sexual Life,* 1980). Dr. Benoit made a French Translation of D.T. Suzuki's *The Doctrine of No-mind.*

Berdyaev, Nicolas (1874-1948): Christian existentialist philosopher. Born into the Russian nobility and in his early years a Marxist, he was exiled by the communist government. In 1924 he established himself in Clarmart, near Paris, where he presided over a philosophical academy. There he, Jacques Maritain, Gabriel Marcel, Sergius Bulgakov and others discussed each other's papers, and no doubt it was there that Swami Siddheswarananda came to know him. The main themes of his many books are freedom, creativity, and eschatolology. *The Destiny of Man* (1937) would be a representative work.

Bhagavad Gītā, The Song of the Lord: For one approaching this work for the first time, the most readable version is *The Song of God: The Bhagavad-Gītā* translated by Swami Prabhavanada and

Christopher Isherwood, with an introduction by Aldous Huxley (Mentor Books). A more scholarly, but by no means pedantic, version is that of Swami Nikhilananda which includes notes and comments (New York, Ramakrishna-Vivekananda Center).

Bhāgavata Purāṇa: Also known as the *Bāgavatam.* A tenth-century work attributed to Vyāsa or his son Śukadeva, it expounds religious truths through stories of saints and seers and particularly the life of Kṛṣṇa. Swami Prabhavananda has translated portions of it under the title *The Wisdom of God* (Hollywood, Vedanta Press).

Bhattatiri, Mepathur Narayana: Author of *Narayaneeyam: Bhāgavata Condensed.* (Translated by Swami Tapasyananda. Madras: Śri Ramakrishna, Math, 1982). Narayana Bhattatiri, a sixteenth century scholar, philosopher, and poet summarized the 18,000 verses of the *Bhāgavata Purāṇa.* Among Devotees of Kṛṣṇa his book is looked upon as sacred, having the power of a *mantra,* and is studied daily as part of their devotional practices.

Brahmananda (Rakhal Chandra Ghosh) (1863-1922): A monastic disciple of Sri Ramakrishna, whom the latter regarded as his spiritual son. As Swami Brahmananda he was for many years the president of the Ramakrishna Order. His disciple, Swami Prabhavananda, expounded on his life and teachings in *The Eternal Companion* (Vedanta Press, Hollywood).

Carmelite Order: The "Order of Our Lady of Mount Carmel" was founded in Palestine c. 1154, though it has claimed continuity with hermits who settled on Mt. Carmel in early times; it has even claimed descent from Elijah and the "sons of the prophets" (II Kings 2). The primitive rule was extremely ascetic, prescribing poverty, solitude, and complete abstinence from flesh. After the failure of the Crusades, many members migrated to Europe. During the sixteenth century the discipline became very relaxed. St. Teresa and her disciple, St. John of the Cross, instituted reforms which restored the primitive rule. The reformed Carmelites (the men are called "White Friars") are known as "Discalced." The "Calced" Carmelites follow a "Mitigated Rule."

Chaitanya (1485-1534): Bengali mystic who abruptly renounced his life as an outstanding scholar to become an ecstatic worshipper of Kṛṣṇa (Vaiṣṇavas regard him as an incarnation of Kṛṣṇa). For him, *Bhakti-Yoga* was the path to God-realization, and japa the most important practice. His ecstatic love embraced all castes and faiths. As a common noun his name means "spiritually awakened consciousness."

Cakras or Chakras: See Kuṇḍalinī Yoga.

Deva: A god, or the male form of a semi-divine being. Capitalized, the word may be added to the name of a God-man to connote reverence (e.g., Chaitanya Deva).

Devī: Goddess. The word often follows the name of a goddess (e.g., Lakṣmī Devī). It is sometimes added to the first name of an Indian lady to connote respect.

Elizabeth of the Trinity (1880-1906): French Carmelite nun and mystic, author of the celebrated hymn "Oh my God, Trinity whom I Adore."

Garrigou-Lagrange, Reginald, OP: He was, with Jacques Maritain, the leader of the twentieth century revival of Thomism. In his *Christian Perfection and Contemplation According to St. Thomas and St. John of the Cross,* he sustains the thesis that Christian perfection consists chiefly in charity, and that infused contemplation of the mysteries of faith is the normal way of sanctity. Incidentally, he also maintains, contrary to Swami Siddheswarananda, that ascetical and mystical theology is not just for the select few. He does not discuss pagans in his book; the Swami is drawing an inference.

Gauḍapāda: The first historic expounder of non-dualistic philosophy. He lived some time before the eighth century. Author of the *Kārikā,* a commentary on the *Māṇḍūkya Upaniṣad.* Śaṁkara said that the *Kārikā* and the *Maṇḍūkya Upaniṣad* together "embody the quintessence of all the *Upaniṣads* and *Vedānta.*"

Gospel of Sri Ramakrishna: See **Gupta**.

Gupta, Mahendranath: Popularly known as "M" (1854-1932). A householder and school principal, versed in Western philosophy. He became a disciple of Sri Ramakrishna and recorded conversations of the Master with various groups during the last four years of his life. These have been translated from Bengali into English by Swami Nikhilananda under the little *The Gospel of Sri Ramakrishna,* published by the Ramakrishna center of New York.

Hriday (1829-18?): Though seven years older than Sri Ramakrishna, he was the latter's nephew and served as his uncle's attendant at the temple of Dakshineswar from 1855-80.

Hui-Neng (683-713): Later known as the sixth Patriarch. He may have been illiterate; in any case, he was not a scholar. Dr.

Suzuki says that from him we may date the birth of Chinese Ch'an (Zen—as distinct from its Indian form). His *Platform Sutra* is a basic Zen text which has been translated by Charles Lux in his *Ch'an and Zen Teachings.*

Jeans, Sir James (1887-1946): British physicist and mathematician. He was the first to propose that matter is continuously created throughout the universe. He wrote both technical and popular works; of the latter, *The Universe Around US* has been widely read.

John of The Cross (1542-91): Spanish Carmelite mystic and poet. He studied theology at Salamanca and was ordained a priest in 1567. Dissatisfied with the laxity of his order, he joined Teresa of Avila in introducing reforms. The General of his order had him imprisoned under conditions of great hardship. He escaped after nine months, though later, as a result of disputes with superiors, he was sent to one of the poorest monasteries where ill treatment hastened his death. He was canonised in 1725 and declared a Doctor of the Church in 1925. (See Bibliographical Notes).

Karman, Theodore Von (1881-1963): Hungarian born research engineer who lived in America after 1930. He was known as the father of supersonic flight.

Latu Maharaj: See Adbhutananda.

Lawrence, Brother (c. 1605-91): Born Nicholas Herman in Lorraine, and later known as Brother Lawrence of the Resurrection, he joined the Carmelite order in 1649 as a lay brother, having previously lived as soldier, servant and hermit. The monastery employed him as a cook. He taught that the soul should keep itself constantly in the divine presence, formal prayer being a continuation of that exercise. After his death his sayings were collected and can be found in numerous English editions under the title *The Practice of the Presence of God.*

Leuba, James H. (1858-1946): American psychologist who tried to give psychological and physiological explanations for mystical experiences.

Lépée, Canon Marcel (1888-1951): Author of three books on St. Teresa, of which one, *Sainte Thérèse d'Avila, le Réalisme Chrétien* (Paris, 1947) is his doctral thesis. None of his books has been translated into English.

"M" (author of Gospel): See **Gupta**.

Māṇḍūkya Upaniṣad: A brief Upaniṣad (twelve verses), for which

Śaṁkara's teacher wrote a *Kārikā* (Commentary) of two-hundred and fifty verses. Śaṁkara wrote a highly philosophical commentary on the Upaniṣad and the *Kārikā*, which have been translated with notes by Swami Nikhilananda. (Calcutta: Advaita Ashram: also contained in Volume II of Swami Nikhilananda's translation of the complete Upaniṣads.) Swami Siddheswarananda agrees with many others who have said that the whole teachings of *Advaita Vedānta* are contained in this Upaniṣad along with its commentaries.

Manu: Literally "Man." A sage of unknown antiquity who incarnated fourteen times. Those incarnations are progenitors and law-givers of the human race. The Laws of Manu (somewhere between the second century B.C.E. and the second century C.E.) have become the canon law of Hinduism and continue to dominate Hindu law.

Mukerji, Dhan Gopal: *The Face of Silence* (New York: E. P. Dutton & Company, 1926). Romain Rolland says of this book that it is "of exceptional value as a work of art" and "a brilliant evocation of the figure of the Master in the atmosphere of India of this time." He adds that "The Ramakrishna Mission has not taken in very good part the liberties due at times to the lively imagination of the artist in the reported words; and it has issued a warning against some of its 'theological interpretations.' "

Nārada: A legendary figure, a "*nitya-siddha*" (one who is eternally perfect). Stories about him are found in the Purāṇas, and among the works ascribed to him are the *Bhakti-Sūtras,* 84 cryptic aphorisms on the love and worship of God. Swami Prabhavananda has translated them under the title *Nārada's Way of Divine Love* (Hollywood Vedanta Society). The Swami has provided lucid commentary.

Pantañjali: A legendary figure about whom nothing is known for certain. Attributed to him are the *Brahma Sūtras,* also known as the *Yoga Sūtras* or *Vedānta Sūtras.* This work consists of 192 aphorisms written some time between the fourth century B.C.E. and the fourth century C.E. These aphorisms are always published with commentary. Swami Vivekananda provided one in his *Rāja-Yoga.* Swami Prabvavananda and Christopher Isherwood collaborated on a version called *How to Know God* (Hollywood, Vedanta Press). (Isherwood lived to regret the choice of that title.)

Prajāpati: "Lord of Creatures." At different periods identified with various gods and the highest manifestation of Brahman. A divinity presiding over procreation and the protector of life.

Prince, Morton (1854-1929): Founder of the Harvard Psychological clinic. He wrote on multiple and co-conscious personalities. His *The Dissociation of a Personality* (1905) analyses a woman with three personalities, one of which undergoes a religious conversion.

Rāma: (*also Rāmacandra*). An incarnation of Vishnu and an ideal king; hero of the epic *Rāmāyaṇa.* He and his wife, Sītā, are venerated as the ideal married couple.

Ramakrishna (1836-86): A God-man or Divine Incarnation whose life inspired the renaissance of modern *Vedānta.* Born into an impoverished Brahmin family and nearly illiterate, he spent most of life as a priest in a Kālī temple near Calcutta. After realizing his union with God through various paths within Hinduism as well as through Christianity and Islam, he proclaimed the Harmony of Religions: ultimate Reality can be known by a follower of any religion if his or her devotion is sufficient. During the last six years of his life he attracted a number of disciples who carried on his teachings, notably Swami Vivekananda.

Rāmānuja (1017-1137): South Indian philosopher-saint, founder of *Viśiṣṭādvaita,* or qualified non-dualism, which teaches that all living creatures and non-living matter are parts of Brahman, who is their soul and controlling power. He wrote commentaries on the *Vedānta Sūtras* and the *Gītā* as well as original philosophical treatises. He stresses *Bhakti-Yoga,* the path of love (rather than Jñāna-Yoga). His "ideas concerning God and the soul bear an astonishing resemblance to ideas on the same subjects with which Scholastic philosophy concerned itself during the Christian Middle Ages." (Swami Prabhavananda)

Ramaṇa Maharṣi (1879-1950): Considered by many the greatest Hindu saint of the twentieth century. At the age of seventeen, without any preparation on his part and without the guidance of any guru, he had a profound experience of his true self and his identity with the absolute. For fifty-four years he lived on the holy hill of Arunachala, where eventually his followers established an āśhram. He wrote little, teaching mainly through answering questions and relentlessly directing his questions to self-inquiry. Swami Siddheswarananda visited him on several occasions.

Rāmprasād (1723-1803): Bengali poet-saint whose fervid songs on the Divine Mother gained great popularity. Sri Ramakrishna was fond of singing them.

Rolland, Romain, (1866-1944): *The Life of Ramakrishna* (Calcutta: Advaita Ashrama, 1928). In 1915 Rolland was awarded the Nobel Prize for literature. Rolland was an historian as well as a novelist and hence is careful about documentation, but he writes with an enthusiasm that becomes lyrical at times. Hence many readers (including your translator), would disagree with Swami Siddheswarananda's assessment. Rolland's *Life of Vivekananda and the Universal Gospel*, is meant as a companion volume to this one; together they have the title *A Study of Mysticism and Action in Living India.*

Śaṁkara (or Shankara or Śaṅkarācārya): Dates assigned to him vary between the sixth and eighth century C.E. A philosopher, poet, scholar, saint, mystic, who in his thirty-two years founded numerous monasteries and composed a great number of commentaries on sacred texts as well as theological works. He has been referred to as the Aquinas of *Vedānta* due to his dialectical skill. Swami Siddheswarananda refers to one of his most important works, the *Viveka chūḍāmaṇi* or "Crest-Jewel of Discrimination" as the basic text on *Advaita Vedānta.* It has been translated by Swami Prabhavananda and Christopher Isherwood (Vedanta Press).

Saradananada, Swami (Sharat Chandra Chakravarti, 1856-1929): *Ramakrishna, the Great Master* (Published by Sri Ramakrishna Math, Madras, in two volumes, translated from the Bengali). This is the standard work to which all serious students of Sri Ramakrishna refer. The author in his youth was trained by Sri Ramakrishna, and he obtained information from the Master's direct disciples and others associated with him. It is more than a biography. The author analyses and meditates on the Master's spiritual experiences. He gives the traditions behind the events of his life. He explains Vedāntic nomenclature. He died before writing an account of the final weeks of the Master's life.

Schweitzer, Albert (1875-1965): Alsacian muscian, theologian, philosopher, and medical doctor. He edited and recorded the organ works of Bach and wrote a definitive interpretation of his music. As a biblical scholar and theologian he made signal contributions to our understanding of Jesus and Paul. He showed how the whole ministry of Jesus was dominated by HIS knowledge of His Messiahship and of the imminent end of the world; Paul's thought likewise was pervaded by the eschatological expectation. As a philosopher he developed an ethic of "reverence for life," including the non-human. He was awarded the Nobel Peace Prize in 1954.

Sūradass (1483-1563): The author of songs celebrating the youthful exploits and loves of Kṛṣṇa. See "Suradas and His Kṛṣṇa-Bhakti' in *Kṛṣṇa: Myths, Rites, and Attitudes*, edited by Milton Singer (1966).

Suzuki, D.T. (1870-1966): A Japanese scholar who is usually credited with introducing Zen Buddhism to the West. Swami Siddheswarananda refers to *The Zen Doctrine of No-Mind, the Singnificance of the Sutra of Hui-Neng (Wei-lang)* (1972, reprinted 1991). (See Hui-Neng)

Teresa of Avila: Also known as Teresa of Jesus (1515-82). Spanish Carmelite nun and mystic. She became a nun in 1533 under a "mitigated observance." After certain mystical experiences (Divine locutions, intellectual visions of Christ) she felt called to found houses in which the primitive rule would be strictly observed. Those who practiced strict observance became known as "Discalced Carmelites" and were violently opposed by the mitigated or "Calced Carmelites." She was greatly assisted by St. John of the Cross. She was canonised in 1622. In 1970 Pope Paul VI elevated her to the rank of Doctor of the Church, the first woman to be so honoured.

Tota Puri: Dates uncertain. A monk of the Śaṁkara Order who, in 1864, initiated Sri Ramakrishna into monastic life and taught him *Advaita* (non-dualistic) *Vedānta.*

Upanishads or Upaniṣads: The best translation is probably that of Swami Nikhilananda, published originally in four volumes by Harper's but now by the Ramakrishna Vedanta Society of New York. It includes thorough explanations and notes; it makes use of the commentaries of Śaṁkarācārya. A one volume abridgement was published as a Harper Torchbook.

Vaishnavism: One of the three principle forms of deity worship in modern Hinduism. Vaiṣṇavites regard Viṣṇu as the supreme being and worship him and his various incarnations, such as Rāma and Kṛṣṇa. Generally their worship is in the form of song and poetry (V. Ālvār and Sūradas) and assumes that an individual can have a direct relationship with God.

Vivekananda: (1863-1902): Narendranath (or Naren) Datta, latter known as Swami Vivekananda. He was the chief disciple of Sri Ramakrishna. In 1893 he represented Hinduism at the World Parliament of Religions in Chicago. That year and in 1899 he lectured widely in America, also in England. His lectures have been collected in eight volumes. He founded the monastic Order of Ramakrishna and also the Ramakrishna Mission, which runs schools, hospitals and clinics, and does relief work, something like the Red Cross. He hoped to help India acquire dignity and self-sufficiency, in part by adopting Western methods, whereas he wished the West to acquire some of the spirituality of the East. He is generally considered to be the interpreter of *Vedānta* for the modern age.

Woodroffe, Sir John (1865-1936): Educated at Oxford, he became professor of law at the University of Calcutta and judge of the city's high court. Later he returned to Oxford where he was reader in Indian law. He researched, translated, and edited tantric texts and published them under the pseudonym Arthur Avalon. Probably best known is *Serpent Power* (Madras: Ganesh and Co, 9th edition, 1973).

Bibliographical Notes by the Translator

1. Carmelites

E. Allison Peers has translated the works of St. Teresa of Avila in separate paperback volumes published by Image Books/Doubleday. He has also translated the complete works of St. John of the Cross in separate volumes, same publisher. All these volumes contain useful introductions and notes.

Kieran Kavanaugh and Otilio Rodriguez have translated the collected works of St. Teresa of Avila and of St. John of the Cross, published by ICS Publications. These also have good introductions as well as helpful indices.

At least three poets have translated the poems of St. John of the Cross; Roy Campbell (Penguin), William Barnstone (New Directions) and John Nims (University of Chicago Press). All these are in bi-lingual texts.

The Autobiography of St. Thérèse of Liseiux has been translated by John Beevers for Image Books.

Antonio De Nicholas has published new translations of selections in *St. John of the Cross, Alchemist of the Soul: His Life, His Poetry,* (bi-lingual), *His Prose* (Paragon House; 1989, foreword by Seyyed Nasr). He agrees with Fr. Garrigou-LaGrange that mystical theology is not just for a select few, contrary to Swami Siddheswarananda. In his book he aims to "recover the lost faculty of imagining so that John's poetry can again be linked authentically to its origins". As one who has been educated in Spain and India, who knows Sanskrit and has written on the Vedas and the *Gītā,* he would himself be competent to write a comparative study such as Swami Siddheswarananda's. He gives a thorough bibliography on St. John of the Cross.

The literature on the Carmelite Saints is enormous. Consult the bibliography mentioned above. I will suggest here a few of the works I have personally found illuminating.

John Welch O. Carm. has written two Jungian studies published by Paulist Press. In *Spiritual Pilgrims: Carl Jung and Teresa of Avila* he compares *The Interior Castle* with the Jungian individuation process. In *When Gods die: An Introduction to John of the Cross* he gives a summary of each of the saint's works followed by "Reflections" which draw on Jung as well as Bernard Lonergan. James Arraj has written *St. John of the Cross and Dr. C.G. Jung* (Tools for Inner Growth, Box 520, Chiloquin, OR 97624). The Author spends many pages on misunderstandings of John of the Cross and problems in relating him to Jung, but he finds in the end that combined they can lead to a renewal of the life of prayer and can be used in the science of spiritual direction. Another psychological comparison has been made by Kevin G. Culligan: "Toward a Contemporary Model of Spiritual Direction: A Comparative Study of St. John of the Cross and Carl Rogers" (*Carmelite Studies* 2, 1982).

Mary Jo Meadow and Kevin Culligan have written "Congruent Spiritual Paths: Christian Carmelite and Theravadan Buddhist Vipassana" in *The Journal of Transpersonal Psychology*, Volume 19, No. 2, 1986.

Pilgrimage and Possession, Conversion in the Writings of St. John of the Cross and St. Teresa by Sister Eileen Mary, SLG (Convent of the Incarnation, Fairacres, Oxford OX4 1TB, England) is particularly interesting for showing a correspondence between the *Interior Castle* and the ancient Chinese philosophy of *I-Ching.*

Louis Lavelle has chapters on Saints Teresa and St. John of the Cross in *Four Saints* (University of Notre Dame Press). Chapter 12 of Ralph Harper's *Human Love, Existential and Mystical* (Johns Hopkins Press) is entitled "Seven Stages of Love" and deals with St. John of the Cross, especially *The Spiritual Canticle.*

I do not know of anyone who has dealt with the subject Swami Siddheswarananda has in his book, although, Swami Nityabodhananda of the Ramakrishna Order has written on "The Bhakti Yoga of John of the Cross" in *Myths and Symbols in Indian Civilization* (Sri Ramakrishna Math, Madras). An American *Vedāntin*, Nancy Pope Mayorga, has written on St. John of the Cross as a *bhakta* in *The Spiritual Athlete* (pp. 141-151), a collection of essays edited by Ray Berry (Olema, CA., Joshua Press).

2. HINDU THOUGHT

Undoubtedly the best short introduction to Hinduism is the chapter with that title in Huston Smith's *The Great Religions* (Harper: San Francisco, 1991). Swami Prabhavananda's *Spiritual Heritage of India* (Vedanta Press) is a good book length treatment (which includes Buddhism, Jainism, etc.).

Ramakrishna and His Disciples by Christopher Isherwood (Vedanta Press) describes the lives and teachings of the men referred to by Swami Siddheswarananda. It is written with clarity and intended for the Western reader unfamiliar with *Vedānta.* A more recent work, *The Great Swan: Meetings with Ramakrishna* (Shambala) creates an evocative dramatic setting for the teachings.

Two collections of Swami Siddheswarananda's essays have been translated from French into English. *Some Aspects of Vedanta Philosophy* includes essays on the Vedas, the Upaniṣads, the *Gītā* and a long essay on "The Ontology of Vedānta." These were lectures given at the University of Toulouse during World War II. *Meditations According to Yoga-Vedanta* includes a Foreword by his lifelong friend, Dr. S. Radhakrishnan. Both books were published by the Sri Ramakrishna Ashrama, Puranttukara.

Glossary of Sanskrit Terms

This list includes only essential terms not fully explained in the text. When a term had different meanings in different schools of thought, only the sense in which Swami Siddheswarananda is using the word is given.

Advaita (Non-dualistic) **Vedānta**: One of the three systems of Vedāntic thought and the most widely known, whose chief exponent is Śaṁkara. It teaches that the manifest universe or creation (*jagat*), embodied souls (*jīvas*), and God (*Brahman*) are ultimately identical. Non-duality is not accessible to reason, for the ego-bound mind in the waking condition cannot step out of the duality of subject-object realationship. "Non-duality" is a more accurate word for this philosophy than "monism," for the latter word implies the idea of unity which in turn implies diversity. *Advaita Vedānta* goes beyond all notions of number and mental concepts which depend on antitheses. See *Māyā.*

Ahaṁkāra: *Aham* = personal pronoun "I". *Kar* = make, do. Hence "I-maker". The ego, the principle of self-consciousness. The component of the mind which claims sense impressions for itself and establishes them as individual knowledge.

Ālvar: A Tamil word meaning "he who rules the world by his love of God and his devotion and self-surrender to God." The Ālvars are Śaivite poet-saints who lived in Tamil Nadu between the fifth and ninth centuries C.E. They were a major influence in the *bhakti* movement; Ramanuja called their works "*The Veda of the Vaishnavas.*" They conceived the whole world as the Body of God and submitted themselves to Him like a woman to her lover, oblivious of everything else.

Ānanda: Absolute joy or bliss. A state of consciousness beyond duality, free from anxiety. Brahman is said to be *sat-cit-ānanda* (being-consciousness-bliss). In the monastic order of Śaṁkara, a *saṁnyasin*'s name always ends in "*ānanda.*" *Viveka* = discrimination.

Vivekananda = one whose bliss is in discrimination.

Ātman: Self or soul. Essence of essence. With capital *A*, the supreme Soul or Brahman. With small *a*, the individual soul. According to *Advaita Vedānta, Ātman* and Brahman are essentially identical.

Brahman: From BRH = to grow. The ultimate principle, creator, maintainer, destroyer of everything in the universe. The Absolute, Eternal, Universal Spirit. Its three attributes are universal being, consciousness, and bliss (*Saccidānanda*). The Universal Principle is called *Ātman* in man and Brahman in the Cosmos, but the two terms designate one and the same ontological reality. The unity of the individual soul and the universal soul is the fundamental theme of the Upaniṣads.

Buddhi: (From Budh, to awaken, recover consciousness. Cf. the Buddha, the enlightened one, the one who has awakened.) Power of forming and retaining conceptions and general notions; the faculty of mind which discerns, judges, comprehends; the discriminative faculty by which doubts are resolved and decisions made.

Causal Body. See Kosha.

Citta. From *Cit* = to perceive, know, appear. Individual consciousness, one aspect of universal mind.

Dharma: From *Dhar* = hold, support, preserve. In the metaphysical sense, it refers to those universal laws of nature that sustain the operation of the manifestation of all things. Applied to the individual, it refers to a code of conduct that sustains the soul and produces virtue, morality, or religious merit.

Gross Body: See Kosha.

Guṇas: Thread, cord, strand, quality, attribute. All things in the manifest world (*prakṛti*) are structurally composed of three *guṇas*. As qualities of *māyā*, they are dependent on Brahman, but they veil the reality of *Brahman.* If they are fully in balance, nothing appears—no creation, no manifestation. Once the balance is disturbed, creation appears. *Sattva* embodies peace, serenity, luminosity, purity. *Rajas* embodies activity, passion, energy, restlessness, also egoism and selfishness. *Tamas* embodies inertia, torpor, heaviness, ignorance. In human development *Sattva* must be realized. *Tamas* is the obstacle to realization. *Rajas* is the force that overcomes *Tamas.* But for the realization of the *ātman, sattva* must be transcended.

Hiraṇyagarbha: Literally, "Golden Egg," formed from the seed deposited by the self-existent Brahman on the eve of creation. The seed took the form of a golden egg out of which Brahman was born as Brahmā, the creator god.

Īśvara: The supreme deity and lord of the universe as personal god, god with attributes of omnipotence, omnipresence, omniscience, possessed of infinite wisdom, strength, virtue, splendour. Same as *saguṇa* Brahman.

Japa: The practice of repeating over and over one of the names of God, usually one's own *mantra*, and sometimes with the aid of a rosary.

Jīva: The embodied self that identifies with body and mind and experiences life and death, pleasure and pain, because of ignorance of its divinity. A *jīvanmukta* is one liberated while still living. Freed from the bond of ignorance, such an one gives up identification with body and mind.

Kali-Yuga: The last of the four *yugas* or ages. A *yuga* is a measurement of time on a cosmic scale. The *Kali-Yuga* began at midnight between the 17th and 18th of February 3102 B.C.E. and endures 423,000 years. At the end of the *Kali-Yuga* the world will be dissolved and the cycle will begin again.

Kāma: Craving, pleasure, lust; but also legitimate desire, fulfilment of which is one of the four fruits of human life.

Kośa or Kosha: Sheath or covering. Five *kośas*, one within another, envelope the *Ātman*, which remains separate from them and unaffected by their properties. Beginning with the outermost *kośa*, they are: (1) *Annamaya-kośa*, the gross physical sheath nourished by food. (2) *Prāṇamnaya-kośa*, the subtle or vital sheath, which holds together body and mind. As long as this vital principle exists in the organism, life continues. Breath is the gross manifestation of this sheath. (3) *Manomaya-kośa*, the sheath of the mind, which receives sense impressions. (4) *Vijñānamaya-kośa*, the sheath of the intellect, refers to the faculty which discriminates or wills. (5) *Ānandamaya-kośa*, the sheath of bliss, nearest the blissful *Ātman*. The first two form the gross frame or body, the second two form the subtle frame or body, and the last the causal frame or body.

Kuṇḍalinī Yoga: A tāntric practice. The spiritual force in every human being is imaged as a serpent power (*kuṇḍalinī*) coiled at the base of the spine. Once awakened, it can ascend through six centres of subtle energy (*cakras*) to the top of the head, at which point the awakened spiritual energy achieves enlightenment (*samādhi*). See *The Serpent* by Arthur Avalon (Sir John Woodroffe).

Mahat: Cosmic Intelligence.

Manas: From "Man": think, believe, imagine, suppose. In the widest sense, all mental powers: intellect, intelligence, understanding, perception, conscience, will. In the more limited sense, a component of the mind which receives sense impressions from the outside world and presents them to the *buddhi.*

Mārga: Road, path, way.

Māyā: Most often translated as "Illusion," but that term is misleading without explanation. The senses are unrealiable, subject to error and distortion, and the world they perceive, the emirical world, is conditioned and transitory. That world has a temporary, uncertain, relative reality called *māyā.* It has two aspects: *avidyā* or ignorance, which leads away from God towards worldiness, materiality, passion, greed; and *vidyā* or knowledge, which leads to God-realization and finds expression in spiritual virtues. Both aspects are in the realm of time, place, and causality and hence are relative. They are transcended by realizing Brahman. From that standpoint, *māyā* is illusion.

Neti, Neti: Literally, "Not this, not this." The process of rejecting appearances of the entire universe as superimposition upon *Brahman.* A process of negative discrimination which leads to the knowledge that *Brahman* alone exists and nothing else.

Nivṛtti-Mārga: The path that returns inward to spiritual self-recollection.

Pitṛ: Literally, father. Plural, ancestors. Refers to: (1) deceased ancestors, to whom food and water are offered on certain occasions; (2) the ten mystical forefather of the human race, the Prajāpatis; and (3) the first sons of the gods.

Pratīkas: Representation.

Prakṛti: Nature. The primal matter of which the universe consists. Its structure is determined by the three *guṇas.* In *Advaita Vedānta,* matter has no final reality, since the material world is experienced only in the waking and dream states, and not in deep sleep or *turīya*: only that which exists in all four states is real.

Pūjā: (Sometimes spelled poojā). Hindu ritualistic worship. It has varying forms but usually involves the use of incense, sandal paste, water, candles and a food offering. It is performed by a *pujārī* (male) or *pujārina* (female).

Rajas: See *Guṇas.*

Ṛṣi or Rishi: Literally, one who has knowledge or sees—a seer. The ṛṣis were legendary founders of Hinduism who communicated the fundamental beliefs and mystical insights that were elaborated upon in later ages. It can also be a general term to refer to saints and poets.

Ṛta or Rita: Literally, "right" or "true." Cosmic order, divine law, righteousness. The living truth that works and flows directly from the divine. A concept basic to Vedic Hinduism, it was replaced in later Hinduism by "*Dharma.*"

Sāṁkhya: The oldest of the six schools of Hindu philosophy and the first to try to harmonize the philosophy of the Vedas through thought. This philosophy teaches that the universe is an eternal process of unfolding, without beginning or end; that the world-order is reason and an expansion of the highest kind of intelligence; that there is no part without an assignable function, value, and purpose. The universe is an evolution of *prakṛti* (primordial nature), which, through its proximity to *puruṣa* (pure consciousness) produces *mahat* (cosmic intelligence), then *ahaṁkāra* (ego-sense), then *buddhi* (discriminative faculty), then *manas* (the recording faculty). There also evolve the five organs of perception, the five organs of action, and the five *tanmātras* (subtle principles which, by combining and recombining produce the five gross elements).

Saṁskāra: From *kara* (action) and *saṁ* (together). An impression, or potentiality created in the mind as a result of an action or thought. The sum total of a person's *saṁskāras* constitutes that person's character.

Satori: A term used in Zen Buddhism to designate a state beyond discrimination and differentiation.

Sattva: See *Guṇas.*

Savikalpa Samādhi: The first stage of transcendental consciousness, in which the distinction between subject and object persists. In this state the spiritual aspirant may have a mystic vision of the Personal God.

Sheath: See *Kosha.*

Subtle Body: See *Kośa.*

Tamas: See *Guṇas.*

Tantra: One of the fundamental elements in the "Eternal

Religion" (*Sanātana Dharma*) of Hinduism . Its central theme is the divine energy and creative power (*śakti*) as represented by the feminine aspect of various gods. Personified as a goddess (*devī*) who is portrayed as the wife of Śiva. Corresponding to the particular form taken by Śiva, his Śakti may be a fortune-granting figure such as Lakṣmī or Gaurī, or it may be a terrifying figure, such as Kālī or Durgā. Two tāntric schools have evolved: the left-hand path, devoted to sexual licentiousness and debauchery, and the right-hand path featuring ritual purification and strict spiritual disciplines. See *Kuṇḍalinī Yoga.* (Tibetan Buddhist Tantra is somewhat different.)

Turīya: Literally, fourth. *Turīya* is the highest state to which a human can aspire, transcending the states of waking, sleep, and deep sleep. It is not a state which comes in the train of the other three; it is a common factor in all states. Scriptures call it the fourth because the aspirant who follows a *sādhanā* according to *Advaita* attains the integral experience, and in the waking state realizes that "All this is Brahman." It is a state of absolute consciousness, beyond thought, causality, or identification with the body; indescribable, indicated by such negations as undetermined, unconditioned, infinite.

Vairājña or Vairāgya: Renunciation of all desires to enjoy the fruit of action, birth here and hereafter. Indifference to the unreal and transitory.

Vedas and Vedānta: The Vedas (from vid, to know) are the oldest known sacred scriptures in the world, to which orthodox Hindus ascribe divine origin and authority. They deal with rituals and knowledge; the knowledge portion being called "Upaniṣads." "*Anta*" means end, *Vedānta* is literally "the end of the Vedas," the concluding, philosophical or theological portions of the Vedas. There are various schools of interpretation. Basically, *Vedānta* teaches that the purpose of life is to realize the ultimate Reality or Godhead, here and now, through spiritual practice. That Reality is called Brahman when regarded as transcendent, *Ātman* when regarded as immanent.

Virāṭ or Virāj: The all-pervading Spirit in the form of the universe.

Yantra: A mystic diagram used as a symbol of the Divine, especially in *tantra.*

Index